I0112480

Discover and Create Meaning in Your Life

Creating and Utilizing Hope for Healing

Dr. Michelle Scallon & Dr. John Liptak

WholePerson
Associates, Inc.

publisher of therapy, counseling, and self-help resources

101 West 2nd Street, Suite 203, Duluth, MN 55802-5004 · WholePerson.com

Whole Person Associates

101 West 2nd Street, Suite 203
Duluth, MN 55802-5004
800-247-6789
Books@WholePerson.com
WholePerson.com

Discover and Create Meaning in Your Life

Printed in the United States of America

Editorial Director: Jack Kosmach
Art Director: Mathew Pawlak
Cover Design: Mathew Pawlak
Editors: Peg Johnson and Adam Sippola

Library of Congress Control Number: 2023942001
ISBN: 978-1-57025-376-8

Introduction

Most research in psychology focuses on all that is negative about human functioning. However, the field of positive psychology takes a different approach, considering how normal people can attain greater happiness, meaning, and purpose in their lives. This new approach to psychology operates on the assumption that what is good in life is just as real as what is bad and that mental health is not merely the absence of mental illness.

One of the founders of the positive psychology movement, Martin Seligman (2008), suggests that life satisfaction is the result of three types of "happy lives" people live:

1. **The Pleasant Life.** A life characterized by cultivating positive emotion. A variety of skills, such as savoring and mindfulness, can amplify these emotions and contribute to this lifestyle.

2. **The Life of Engagement.** A life characterized by flow. In this life, people spend as much of their time as possible involved in activities (work, parenting, leisure, etc.) that are so engaging that they lose track of time.

3. **The Meaningful Life.** A life characterized by a deep sense of meaning. In this life, people find greater meaning by using their strengths to belong to and be of service to something larger than themselves.

While these lives may all result in different types of well-being, Seligman's research indicates that the meaningful life is the strongest contributor to overall life satisfaction. This workbook focuses on helping participants lead meaningful lives.

Positive Psychology and the Study of Meaning

Throughout modern history, humans have been obsessed with asking one question, "What is the meaning of life?" All people strive for a sense of meaning, a worthwhile purpose, and the feeling that life is worth more than the sum of its parts. Some believe people can find meaning in every scenario, event, occurrence, and context. People can find meaning in pain, suffering, absurd situations, flow, and extreme purpose. People intuitively know that they want meaning in their lives and that meaning helps them thrive and flourish. But what is meaning? Reker and Wong (1988a) define personal meaning as "the cognizance of order, coherence, and purpose in one's existence, the pursuit and attainment of worthwhile goals, and an accompanying sense of fulfillment" (1988b). Similarly, Ackerman (2018) described the positive psychology view of meaning in life. She said that people strive to lead meaningful lives.

- **People can find meaning all around them in the world.**
- **People can create their own sense of meaning.**
- **People can uncover their own unique sense of meaning.**

Positive Psychology researchers throughout the years have discovered that while negative events may decrease happiness, paradoxically, they may increase the meaning in life. People who experience traumatic or emotional experiences build character and learn lessons that make them more compassionate and give us a deeper understanding of themselves and others. Ackerman's study also indicates that people with a purpose and meaningful goals for helping others rated their life satisfaction higher – even when they felt down and out – than those with no life purpose. Having meaning in life is often related to being of service to others. Positive psychologists believe that people who pursue meaning often experience more long-term life satisfaction than those who seek happiness. People who make their lives more meaningful will enjoy the following benefits:

- They will live healthier lives.
- They will exhibit energy and vitality.
- They will be better able to cope with adversity.
- They will be more productive.
- They will experience increased life satisfaction.
- They will be more self-confident and feel better about who they are.
- They will be able to achieve the flow state and feel "at one" with what they are doing.
- They will be able to satisfy their human need for value.

The Search for Meaning

Viktor Frankl's (2006) research and study on meaning laid the foundations for the positive psychology research on meaning that has occurred more recently. Frankl developed a theoretical framework and theory of psychotherapy referred to as logotherapy. Frankl said that a person's search for meaning is the primary motivation in life, not a "secondary rationalization" of instinctual drives. Frankl offered three main concepts to frame the logotherapy approach:

1. Freedom of will.
2. A will to meaning.
3. The meaning of life.

Frankl proposed that a lack of meaning underpins some of the problems he perceived in his time that remain issues today, such as violence, addiction, depression, and suicide. Rather than ignoring existential quandaries, Frankl encouraged people to find, create, or uncover their own meaning, which is personal and often changing. Personal meaning, according to Frankl, could be discovered in three different ways: by creating a work or doing a deed, by experiencing something or encountering someone, and by the attitude people take toward unavoidable suffering.

"In 1998, Dr. Martin Seligman used his inaugural address as the incoming president of the American Psychological Association to shift the focus from mental illness and pathology to studying what is good and positive in life. From this point in time, theories and research examined positive psychology interventions that help make life worth living and how to define, quantify, and create well-being (Rusk & Waters, 2015)." (Madeson, 2017a). Seligman used Frankl's work in developing his positive psychology approach, referred to as the PERMA model. "Seligman selected five components that people pursue because they are intrinsically motivating and they contribute to wellbeing. These elements are pursued for their own sake and are defined and measured independently of each other (Seligman, 2012). Additionally, the five components include both eudaimonic and hedonic components..." (Madeson, 2017b).

Seligman created the PERMA model in which PERMA is an acronym for the following five elements of well-being:

- **Positive Emotions:** Experiencing optimism and gratitude about your past, contentment in the present, and hope for the future.
- **Engagement:** Achieving "flow" with enjoyable activities and hobbies.
- **Relationships:** Forming social connections with family and friends.
- **Meaning:** Finding a purpose in life larger than you. A sense of meaning or purpose plays a pivotal role in finding a purpose in life larger than you. A sense of meaning or purpose plays a pivotal role in a person's level of happiness and fulfillment. Many find ultimate value in their religious or spiritual beliefs, while others focus on helping others, serving a cause greater than themselves, or pursuing creative arts. Those who take time to discover their strengths and abilities often find greater meaning and happiness.
- **Accomplishments:** The pursuit and achievement of goals and successes.

People can find greater meaning in their lives by exploring the activities in each of the chapters of this workbook:

⇨ **Chapter 1: Meaning in Ten Minutes**
⇨ **Chapter 2: Make Meaning by Taking Action**
⇨ **Chapter 3: Discover Meaning Through Mental Health Fitness**
⇨ **Chapter 4: Meaning Through Establishing Self-Worth**
⇨ **Chapter 5: Make Meaning by Doing Things for Others**

The Workbook's Theoretical Orientation

This workbook is based on Scallon and Liptak's (2021) research on the best ways to develop hope to enhance well-being and build resilience. Their positive psychology theory, called the Hierarchy of Hope, leads to hope-based resilience. The Hierarchy of Hope is a model for helping people generate hope and create a new purpose after experiencing significant or traumatic changes. These changes are pivotal events called "Pivot Points." The Hierarchy of Hope demonstrates how to evolve hope into a lifestyle by teaching how to view pivot points as opportunities for growth and meaning, set goals to prompt action, and teach perseverance skills. The following suggestions provide a brief overview for practitioners unfamiliar with the theory.

Concepts of the Hierarchy of Hope Theory

The following are the basic premises of the Hierarchy of Hope (HOH):

- Everyone's Hierarchy of Hope will be different. Everyone has changes that occur in life and peak/pivotal experiences. They make sense of personal change or global affairs in different ways.

- Hope can help people cope during times of change. Encouraging individuals to develop new meaning after stressful situations helps them stay positive.

- It is possible to have hope during times of global or personal change. Life is filled with change. Some changes are more prominent, and some are smaller. All people have control over how they conceptualize their changing life experiences. People can turn any change into positivity and hopefulness. They can capitalize on their strengths when discovering the meaning of their change. Hope provides a sense of certainty during times of change.

- People develop hope when they define positive, new meanings in their lives. Any life change can become an opportunity to create hope and new meanings. People must use different methods to increase hope, depending on their needs at any given time.

- People must draw on their most valuable assets—their personalities—to maintain hopefulness and goals.

- People can evolve hope from a feeling to a lifestyle reflected in all they think, do, and are. People must make hope a vital part of their everyday life.

- Hope depends on eliminating negative habits and experimenting with ideas and actions that make life better and more joyful.

- How people choose to live represents their values and how they reflect their experiences into the world. People live by how they make sense of their changing experiences.

Steps in the Therapeutic Process

Facilitators working with people using the Hierarchy of Hope theory can use the following process or integrate the process into their theoretical approach:

Step 1: Explore Pivot Points

The first goal is to normalize the participant's experience in a non-judgmental way that allows them to express their experiences in the best way they know. Facilitators can help participants identify, explore, and understand the pivot point that brought about personal or global changes impacting their lives. Facilitators can help participants explore these pivot points to derive new and hopeful meaning.

Pivot points represent essential changes in life. These significant events require participants to reflect, pivot, and think in new and innovative ways. Each of the pivots represents ways participants develop new meaning in life. After pivot points, participants can increase their hope and positivity and begin to regain control of their lives. Examples of pivot points include graduating from school, getting your first job, getting married or divorced, losing a loved one, having a child, getting promoted, global crises, and environmental emergencies. The good news is that participants can successfully adjust to pivot points by completing the activities and assessments in this workbook series. The Hierarchy of Hope helps participants draw on their change experiences to identify goals constructively, create new meaning, and restructure their lives.

Hope interventions focus on improving the level of happiness, joy, well-being, and positive cognition through carefully selected strategies. According to Edey, Jevne, and Westra (1998), hope interventions are particularly valuable for clients with four primary concerns:

- The skidding effect – People experience a loss of control.
- The bruising effect – People experience a sense of hopelessness from failure or loss.
- The boomerang effect – People have tried everything to make changes yet find themselves back where they started.
- The alien effect – People feel like no one understands them and find it difficult to connect with others.

How To Explore Pivot Points?

Facilitators can ask questions to understand each participant's perspective about the changes happening in their lives:

    a. How does the client describe the changes occurring in their life? What is the presenting issue?

    b. What is the developmentally appropriate language the client uses, and how does the client best express themself?

    c. Is the pivot point a personal or global change (i.e., the COVID Pandemic)?

    d. How does the client believe the pivot point is affecting their life?

    e. How does the client want the pivot point to improve their life?

    f. How did it prompt the inclusion of negative habits into the person's lifestyle? Can we take out negative habits?

    g. How is the client experiencing change (job, personal, relationship, control, meaning, etc.)?

    h. How can the client create new meaning from this experience (e.g., a shift in priorities) to maintain hope?

    i. How has thinking interfered with the client's ability to move forward?

    j. How has the client conceptualized this change? How has this pivot point changed the client's perspective on life?

    k. Why has the client been reluctant to change?

    l. How can the client be more proactive in meeting their needs?

    m. How are the client's priorities shifting? How does this new meaning result in a different priority for their needs?

Step 2: Therapeutic Process – Facilitators use the workbooks in *Positive Psychology – The Hope Series (The Hope Series)* as a therapeutic process to help participants restructure their goals and implement them to enhance hope.

In Step 2, facilitators help participants regain hope in life. Facilitators help participants see the possibilities, opportunities, options, and alternatives in their lives. Facilitators accomplish this by using the five workbooks in this series to set goals in each of the goal areas.

> **Control:** Increase the participant's experience of positive, hopeful emotions to feel a sense of control in life.
>
> **Meaning:** Help participants increase their sense of meaning, purpose, and self-confidence.
>
> **Accomplishment:** Help participants feel a sense of accomplishment by reflecting on past successes and exploring options and possibilities for future success. Accomplishment enhances self-esteem, confidence, and appreciation of self.
>
> **Relationships:** Help participants build and maintain healthy, hopeful, positive relationships with others.
>
> **Engagement:** Help participants identify and develop that at which they excel.

Step 3: Expect Positive Outcomes

In Step 3, facilitators help people evolve hope from a feeling into a lifestyle. Because people encounter challenges, barriers, and obstacles in implementing their goals, they need help maintaining motivation, perseverance, and effort.

The Workbook's Additional Theoretical Orientations

While the chapters of this workbook are based on the Hierarchy of Hope, the authors used many additional theoretical orientations, including the following evidenced-based practices:

- Cognitive Behavioral Therapy (Beck, 1967)
- Dialectic Behavioral Therapy (Linehan, 1993)
- Acceptance and Commitment Therapy (Hayes & Lillis, 2012)
- Behavioral Activation (Lewinsohn & Shaffer, 1971)
- Interpersonal Therapy (Klerman, DiMascio, Weissman, Prusoff, & Paykel, 1974)
- Hope Theory in Positive Psychology (Snyder, Irving, & Anderson, 1991)

Using the Workbook Series

This workbook series is designed for qualified personnel working with individual clients or groups. The series is flexible for use in a broad range of settings, including, but not limited to: schools, outpatient and inpatient mental health treatment centers, correctional institutions, healthcare facilities, occupational environments, relapse prevention programs, or other relevant settings.

The Hope Series is designed to help people focus on the positive aspects of their lives rather than the negative ones. Positive psychology focuses on helping people build a life filled with hope, meaning, joy, and resilience. It is about assisting people in meeting their needs to move from surviving to flourishing. Positive psychology asks:

- How can people live a good life?
- How can people improve their lives?
- How can people find joy in their lives?
- How can people capitalize on their strengths?

The positive psychology approach is unique and allows for tremendous facilitator flexibility. The five workbooks in *The Hope Series* include:

> *Discover and Create Meaning in Your Life*
> *Generate a Sense of Accomplishment in Your Life*
> *Maintain Positive, Healthy Relationships in Your Life*
> *Regain Control in Your Life*
> *Cultivate Hope and Engagement in your Life*

There is no prescribed order that the workbooks follow. Facilitators may choose to utilize workbooks that represent the most significant needs of the program population with whom they work. Facilitators have further flexibility in using individual chapters within all five workbooks. You may use the workbooks in any sequential order, depending on the needs of your client or group.

The Layout of the Workbooks

This workbook series provides an outcomes-based program that will help facilitators track and asses participant progress, ensure learning objectives are met, and provide valuable data for program evaluation and justification.

Each workbook contains three sections designed to help facilitators use the program materials effectively, explore pre-test and post-test options, and ensure participant growth and development.

1. Assessment

The Hope Scale is included in the Introduction of each workbook. The Hope Scale helps gather information about participants' level of hope before conducting a session using the workbook materials and then again at the end of the process. This pre-test and post-test information can be valuable in assessing each participant's or group's progress. Statistics related to the development of the Hope Scale means and standard deviations and the t-test results of studies using the Hope Scale with Hierarchy of Hope materials are included in the Introduction.

2. Therapeutic Plans

This workbook series relies on therapeutic plans as a daily guide. Therapeutic plans can be lesson plans or treatment plans, depending on the setting in which you work. The G.A.D.E. model is used throughout this workbook series. The therapeutic plans will include the following.

> **Goals:** What do you want participants to be able to do, know, or understand by the end of treatment?
>
> **Actions:** How will you break down the substance of the plan to help participants reach the goal?
>
> **Demonstrations of Learning:** How will you and the participants know if they have achieved the goal?
>
> **Environment:** What do you physically need to do to facilitate the therapeutic process?

Therapeutic plans will contain activities to help participants reflect on previous behaviors, explore emotions, and learn new skills.

3. Journaling

A critical component of this workbook series is journaling. Journaling is critical in enhancing mental health, developing better communication skills, achieving goals, and increasing self-reliance and resilience. People journal by writing about their feelings, thoughts, indulgences, and insights into their lives and beliefs. Facilitators may ask the participants to keep journals, understanding that they will share their journals with the facilitator. Facilitators have three options for evaluating participant journals:

1. Facilitator can provide feedback only.
2. Facilitator can provide feedback with a "Pass" or "Fail."
3. Facilitator can create an objective scoring rubric if they want to provide grades.

Facilitators can choose an option based on their specific needs and circumstances. Facilitators can use journaling as a window into how participants think about what they are learning. Journaling requires more profound self-discovery and promotes the development of wisdom by exploring how to implement what is discovered and learned. Journals are an important source of information about learning difficulties, misconceptions, strengths and weaknesses, and metacognition. Transferring thoughts, ideas, and feelings into written words encourages participants to examine their thought processes. It is a personal record of thoughts that provides a safe communication method and gives facilitators insight into participants' thoughts.

As journals rapidly become the heart of many life skills programs in schools and counseling centers, they promote introspection and the development of wisdom (introspection put into action in daily life). The journaling prompts included in this workbook series will rely on three levels of journaling prompts and entries.

Level 1: The journaling prompts will encourage self-discovery by asking participants to analyze central concepts of what they have learned by referring to the lesson-plan materials for justification. They will be more simplistic to ensure participants understand the presented materials.

Level 2: The reflective journaling prompts will help participants develop metacognitive skills by reflecting on what they learned and how they learned it. These are second-level journaling questions.

Level 3: The journaling prompts will promote the development of wisdom by asking participants to implement metacognitive skills in their daily lives. Because they create wisdom, these are the highest-level journaling prompts.

These journaling prompts will be a private conversation between facilitator and participant. Facilitators will be encouraged to provide feedback through written conversations, questions, notes in the margin, or some notation that lets participants know they are reading and thinking about their entries. In addition, facilitators can grade answers from the prompts to track progress if they choose to.

To the Participants

If you are like most people, global changes over the last few years have influenced how you are living your life. Despite worldwide challenges, there have been a lot of positive impacts. This book is designed to help participants recognize and gain resilience. Resilience is when you recognize the strength inside of you and succeed despite obstacles. These exercises are designed to help you recognize your strengths and remind you of what you have gained over the past few years:

- Many people connected or reconnected with loved ones.
- Some people have turned difficulties into triumphs.
- Some people have created new meaning in their lives out of global change.
- People began to understand the importance of personal hygiene and make positive lifestyle changes.
- Many people made career shifts.
- Many people learned how to make working from home a positive experience for themselves and their families.
- People had time to reflect on their lives and discover hidden knowledge, skills, and abilities.
- Some people rediscovered hobbies and leisure activities they had not pursued for a long time.

We conceived of this workbook using a positive psychology perspective. Positive psychology is concerned with enhancing and utilizing your resiliency. We designed this workbook to help you explore vital thoughts, feelings, and behaviors that can help you be your best self in the post-pandemic era. This workbook series teaches skills in five basic positive psychology areas: Meaning, Relationships, Control, Engagement, and Accomplishment.

We hope you enjoy the activities, assessments, and journaling exercises in this workbook. As you work on the various activities, please remember there are no correct answers. We simply want you to celebrate your strengths. Please take your time and consider your experience as an investment in yourself and your growth and development.

We hope the activities are fun to complete and a positive experience for you. Enjoy the process!

Sincerely,
Dr. Michelle J. Scallon and Dr. John Liptak

Research and Statistics

The next section contains The Hope Scale (Leutenberg & Liptak, 2016) and related statistical research and development data. Facilitators needing evidence of their program's validity and reliability in enhancing hope in participants may use The Hope Scale along with the materials from this workbook series. The data from multiple three-week research studies are included.

A printable version of The Hope Scale and other exercises in this workbook are included in your digital download at https://WholePerson.com/store/DiscoverandCreateMeaning2001.html

The Hope Scale
By Ester Leutenberg & John J. Liptak, EdD

Name _____ Date _____

Hope is a feeling of expectation, belief, and/or desire for a certain thing to happen or to be the case. People who have hope believe that there will be positive things happening in their future. Rather than sitting back and hoping for good things to happen, they take steps to ensure things work out in their favor.

Directions

This scale contains 3 sections of 6 statements each. Read each of the statements and decide whether the statement describes you or not. If the statement describes you, circle the number in the Describes Me column next to that item. If the statement does not describe you, circle the number in the Does Not Describe Me column next to that item.

In the following examples, the circled 2 indicates the person completing the scale believes the statement describes him or her.

Optimistic Attitude (OA) Statements

	Describes Me	Does Not Describe Me
I am an optimistic person	(2)	1
I surround myself with optimistic people	(2)	1

**This is not a test. Since there are no right or wrong answers,
do not spend too much time thinking about your answers.
Be sure to respond to every statement.**

Hope Scale

Name _____ Date _____

Optimistic Attitude (OA) Statements

	Describes Me	Does Not Describe Me
I am an optimistic person	2	1
I surround myself with optimistic people	2	1
I am hopeful about the future even when life is difficult	2	1
I see the glass as half-full	2	1
I try to stay positive even though things aren't going well at the moment	2	1
I am able to see many possibilities in my future	2	1

Scale OA Total _____

Goal Orientation (GO) Statements

	Describes Me	Does Not Describe Me
I set clear short-term everyday goals	2	1
I set reasonable goals	2	1
I have multiple strategies for reaching my goals	2	1
I set long-term goals to work toward	2	1
I prioritize my goals	2	1
I set a new goal once I have achieved my goal	2	1

Scale GO Total _____

Positive Outcomes (PO) Statements

	Describes Me	Does Not Describe Me
I consider different ways to achieve a positive outcome	2	1
I expect to have positive outcomes for the goals I set	2	1
I do not let unexpected situations stop me from reaching my goal	2	1
I am motivated, even when the going gets tough	2	1
I bounce back when I am faced with a setback	2	1
I do not give up until I have completed a task	2	1

Scale PO Total _____

Scoring Directions

The Hope Scale you just completed is designed to measure how much hope you have in your life. On the previous page, total the scores you circled and transfer that number below. Place each number on the continuum line of the matching scale below to find your level of the three aspects of hope.

OA Optimistic Attitude   Total = _____

GO Goal Orientation   Total = _____

PO Positive Outcomes   Total = _____

Profile Interpretation

SCALE OA – Optimistic Attitude

This scale measures a person's mental attitude with the tendency to have a favorable view on situations in life and to see the most favorable options.

6 = Low   **9 = Moderate**   **12 = High**

SCALE GO – Goal Orientation

This scale measures a person's desire to set and work toward personal and professional goals. Goal-oriented people can see what they are trying to achieve clearly and vividly in their minds.

6 = Low   **9 = Moderate**   **12 = High**

SCALE PO – Positive Outcomes

This scale measures a person's attitude of expecting favorable options with the desire to pursue, grow, and succeed in their endeavors.

6 = Low   **9 = Moderate**   **12 = High**

© 2024 WHOLE PERSON ASSOCIATES, 101 WEST 2ND STREET, SUITE 203, DULUTH MN 55802 • 800-247-6789 • WHOLEPERSON.COM

Research & Development

This section outlines the stages involved in the development of the Hope Scale (Leutenberg & Liptak, 2016). The research & development section includes guidelines for development, norm development, and testing.

Guidelines for Development

The Hope Scale was developed to fill the need for a quick, reliable instrument to help people assess their current level of hope. The assessment consists of three scales, each containing six items that explore the respondent's hopeful attitude, goal orientation, and expectations about future success. The Hope Scale also provides teachers and therapists with information that they can use to help people start their path to greater levels of hope.

The Hope Scale was administered to people from a variety of cultural backgrounds. Table 1 shows the results of this study.

Table 1: Means and Standard Deviations (N = 72)

Scales	Mean	SD
Optimistic Attitude	9.85	1.08
Goal Orientation	9.74	1.31
Positive Outcomes	9.78	1.19

Experimental Pre-Test/Post-Test Design Research

The basic premise behind the pre-test/post-test design involves administering The Hope Scale before the hope treatment, followed by administering The Hope Scale again. Pre-test/post-test designs are employed in experimental and quasi-experimental research and can be used with or without control groups. For example, quasi-experimental pre-test/post-test designs may or may not include control groups, whereas experimental pre-test/post-test designs must include control groups. Furthermore, despite the versatility of these designs, they still have limitations, including threats to internal validity. Although such threats are of particular concern for quasi-experimental designs, experimental designs also contain threats to internal validity.

John Liptak administered The Hope Scale in three separate studies (www.hopebasedresilience.com). The results of these studies indicate that levels of hope were significantly increased in both teens and adults in three weeks. The next section describes the results of the studies.

Study 1

The Hope Scale was administered as a pre-test and a post-test to a group of teens who then had the training to enhance their level of hope. These teens were exposed to treatment materials related to the Hierarchy of Hope (http://www.hopebasedresilience.com) for approximately three weeks. The researcher used a 95% Confidence Interval of the Difference. Table 2 shows the results of this study. As can be seen from Table 2, the scores were statistically significantly different at the 99% Confidence Level.

Table 2: A Study of Hope Training (N = 21)

Pairs	Degree of Freedom	One-Sided P	Two-Sided P
OA-OA2	20	<.001	<.001
GO-GO2	20	<.001	<.001
PO-PO2	20	<.001	<.001

Differences in Scores:

As shown in Table 3, teens' scores on each of the three scales were statistically significantly better from the first administration of the Hope Scale to the second administration.

Table 3: Paired Sample Statistics

Scale 1: Optimistic Attitude	Scale 2: Goal Orientation	Scale 3: Positive Outcomes
OA Pre-Test = 8.95	GO Pre-Test = 9.09	PO Pre-Test = 9.10
OA Post-Test = 10.72	GO Post-Test = 10.67	PO Post-Test = 10.43

Study 2

The Hope Scale was then administered to a second group of international teens to determine the reproducibility of the results. The researcher used a 95% Confidence Interval of the Difference. Table 4 shows the results of this study. As can be seen from Table 4, the scores from this group of teens were also statistically significant.

Table 4: A Study of Hope Training (N = 15)

Pairs	Degree of Freedom	One-Sided P	Two-Sided P
OA-OA2	14	<.001	<.001
GO-GO2	14	<.002	<.004
PO-PO2	14	<.004	<.007

Differences in Scores:

As shown in Table 5, teens' scores on each of the three scales were statistically significantly better from the first administration of the Hope Scale to the second administration.

Table 5: Paired Sample Statistics

Scale 1: Optimistic Attitude	Scale 2: Goal Orientation	Scale 3: Positive Outcomes
OA Pre-Test = 9.20	GO Pre-Test = 8.87	PO Pre-Test = 9.20
OA Post-Test = 10.53	GO Post-Test = 10.33	PO Post-Test = 10.40

Study 3

The Hope Scale was administered as a pre-test and a post-test to a group of unemployed adults who then had the training to enhance their level of hope. These adults were exposed to treatment materials related to the Hierarchy of Hope (www.hopebasedresilience.com) for approximately three weeks. The researcher used a 95% Confidence Interval of the Difference. Table 6 shows the results of this study. As can be seen from Table 6, the scores were statistically significantly different at the 99% Confidence Level.

Table 6: A Study of Hope Training (N = 35)

Pairs	Degree of Freedom	One-Sided P	Two-Sided P
OA-OA2 Adults	34	<.001	<.001
GO-GO2 Adults	34	<.001	<.001
PO-PO2 Adults	34	<.001	<.001

Differences in Scores:

As shown in Table 7, adults' scores on each of the three scales were statistically significantly better from the first administration of the Hope Scale to the second administration.

Table 7: Paired Sample Statistics for Adults

Scale 1: Optimistic Attitude	Scale 2: Goal Orientation	Scale 3: Positive Outcomes
OA Pre-Test = 9.49	GO Pre-Test = 9.62	PO Pre-Test = 9.57
OA Post-Test = 10.31	GO Post-Test = 10.60	PO Post-Test = 10.63

Table of Contents

Table of Contents

CHAPTER 1

Meaning in Ten Minutes

Chapter 1 Therapeutic Plan

Goals
- Participants will learn strategies for creating meaning using ten-minute exercises to improve their mood and create meaning in their lives.
- Participants will learn how to create meaning using their time, create new goals, reflect on their past, use their senses, and celebrate their accomplishments.
- Participants will create meaning in their lives by teaching others something new, by using humor, and by understanding how they want to be remembered by others.

Actions
- Facilitators will explain and lead discussions about which ten-minute activities help them create meaning in their lives.
- Facilitators should use each classroom, group situation, or one-on-one client session to structure and administer one or more worksheets to participants.
- Allow participants plenty of time to complete the worksheet.
- Participants can get into smaller groups or pairs to discuss their responses to the activities.
- At this time, participants can move into the larger group to provide opportunities to share their findings. Please remind all participants that they do not have to share anything they do not want to discuss. This space provides room for individuals to reflect; however, there is no obligation to do so.
- Individuals can share their self-discoveries with a trusted professional.

Demonstrations of Learning
- Journaling activities will help determine how much your participants have learned and if they have achieved their goals.
- Journaling activities at the end of each chapter should be given as homework assignments. Facilitators can administer the journaling activities near the beginning (Level 1 Journaling), in the middle (Level 2 Journaling), and near the end (Level 3 Journaling).
- As stated in the Introduction, facilitators can determine if and how to grade the journal entries.

Environment
- Move the seats into a large group, then break into smaller groups or pairs as necessary. When working with an individual client, create a comfortable, neutral environment.
- Download and print exercises from the workbook that are related to your specific topics.

Ten Minutes of Your Time

As strange as it sounds, focusing on one task for ten minutes may be more meaningful than focusing on ten tasks throughout the day. Psychologists often help people improve their mood by activity scheduling, which helps people track their moods and notice they feel better when accomplishing something. Therapists also use behavioral activation, which helps people feel better when they accomplish tasks. This exercise will help you experiment with ten minutes of meaning.

Start by picking one task to accomplish that provides your life with meaning. *For example, maybe you want to become a nurse, so you will spend ten minutes today filling out a school application.*

Follow the instructions below and then answer the questions that follow.

1. Write down a ten-minute task that brings your life meaning. *For example, helping a neighbor carry out the trash, donating money online, or calling an old friend.*

2. Engage in the task after setting a timer for ten minutes.
    ☐ Place a checkmark here when you have done this.

3. Answer the questions below.

What did you accomplish in ten minutes?

_____

_____

Rate your mood while completing the ten-minute task (0=Low, 10 = Best Ever). Why did you rate yourself the way you did?

_____

_____

What did you think when you completed your task?

_____

_____

How do you feel now that you have completed your task?

_____

_____

Ten Minutes of Color

It is amazing what a touch of color can do for you and your mood. This exercise will harness colors to help you make meaning in ten minutes. Researchers have shown that colors can help lift your mood. For example, if you wear a bright sweater that makes you feel happy, you can instantly have a good day. Or, if you add a pillow to your home decor, perhaps this color can create meaning for you. Maybe you have a colorful blanket on your couch in the fall or spring, which helps you feel warm and cozy.

Spend the next few minutes looking through your closet. Pick out an outfit to wear this week with colors that bring meaning to your life. For example, you may choose a brightly colored fall jacket, meaning you will feel inspired to enjoy time outside. Perhaps you will choose an earth-toned outfit, which means you will feel calm and grounded for your office meeting.

1. Set a timer for ten minutes. Look through your closet and pick out the color of an outfit that makes you feel fabulous.
    ☐ Put a checkmark here when you have done this.

2. Try on the outfit in your favorite color.
    ☐ Put a checkmark here when you have done this.

3. What feelings arise when you put on your new outfit?

    _____

    _____

Look around your living or work environment. Notice the colors around you. Think about what kinds of colors make you feel warm and cozy. Think about what colors bring you the happiest memories. Remember what colors bring you joy, and write the associated memory down.

_____

_____

_____

Set a timer and spend ten minutes adding one item of color to your living or work environment that makes you feel good.
    ☐ Put a checkmark here when you have done this.

What feelings or moods do you have now that you have added a touch of color to your environment?

_____

_____

_____

Ten Minutes of Oxygen

The world can feel and look different when you are outside. Our bodies are meant to be outside, breathing fresh, crisp air. One of the most important things you can do is give yourself fresh oxygen outside. Fresh air helps your body relax and helps the blood flow more easily to your brain. Oxygen helps you concentrate, feel better, and improve your mood state. This exercise will help you feel better immediately by allowing you to breathe better. ***Follow the instructions below and then answer the questions regarding getting more air. When your body has more oxygen, your brain functions more efficiently to make better meaning.***

1. The first step is to get outside (if the air quality is good). If the air quality is safe and clean in your area, step outside.
   ☐ Put a checkmark here when you have done this.

2. Once you are outside, take a ten-minute walk. While walking, breathe in the fresh air deeply, reminding yourself of all you are grateful for. Be sure to take several deep breaths while on your ten-minute walk.
   ☐ Put a checkmark here when you have done this.

3. Come back inside after a ten-minute (or longer) walk. Answer the following questions:

How do you feel after your walk?

_____

_____

What are your thoughts after walking?

_____

_____

What was the best part of the walk?

_____

_____

Where did you choose to walk and why?

_____

_____

Did you walk alone or with someone else? Why?

_____

_____

Did this walk help you process anything in your life, helping you to create new meaning?

_____

Ten Minutes of Gratitude

This exercise will help you create meaning by expressing your gratitude. When we recognize what we are thankful for, we develop new perspectives and see things in a new way. When we are grateful, the meaning of any situation can turn around and become more positive.

In this exercise, you will list all of the things you are grateful for from the letters A-Z. Explain what meaning this person, place, or thing brings to your life.

For example, I am grateful for (A) My friend Alicia. She brings humor to my life. She is very loyal and makes me feel good when we speak.

A _____

B _____

C _____

D _____

E _____

F _____

G _____

H _____

I _____

J _____

K _____

L _____

M _____

N _____

O _____

P _____

Q _____

R _____

S _____

T _____

U _____

V _____

W _____

X _____

Y _____

Z _____

Ten Minutes of Appreciation

This exercise will help you create meaning in your life by learning to appreciate the people, places, and things you most admire as you express gratitude through written or spoken words. ***For the next ten minutes, take time to call someone, email somebody, or write a handwritten note to someone to express your appreciation of them.***

Before you send your thank you note, use the prompts that follow to practice what you will say.

Dear _____,

I am writing to express my gratitude for the following:

_____

_____

You have added meaning to my life by:

_____

_____

The adjectives I would use to describe your act of kindness are:

_____

_____

I want to give back by doing the following:

_____

_____

I will always remember what you did because:

_____

_____

I will pay it forward by doing the following:

_____

_____

My other additional words of appreciation are:

_____

_____

Now, call, email, or write to your person.

Ten Minutes of Rap

Rap music is a creative way to express your thoughts and feelings. It is a great way to discover meaning by telling a story. You may not feel you know how to rap, but anyone with a story to tell can rap. ***Uncover and create meaning in the next ten minutes by sharing your story.***

Rap is poetry. The guidelines for creating a rap are below. Some rappers use different terminology.

1. Begin by thinking of something you want to tell people about your life. Think of a cool story, a struggle you overcame, or an inspirational theme you want to tell an audience.
2. Next, write down your story in 16 bars or lines.
3. Rhyme words two at a time at the end of the lines. For example, *"I got my start in baseball as a kid. All I could do was practice, and I did. My coach was sure to be a mentor to me. He helped me feel better so I could see."*
4. Write four lines at a time. The first four bars should include images, the second four lines should include other people's feelings or reactions, the next four lines tell how you made it out of your circumstances, and the last four lines tell the story of what success you felt after overcoming the odds. Next, share your rap with your counselor, friend, or the group. Be sure to use appropriate images and words.

1. _____
2. _____
3. _____
4. _____
5. _____
6. _____
7. _____
8. _____
9. _____
10. _____
11. _____
12. _____
13. _____
14. _____
15. _____
16. _____

How did others react to your rap?

_____

_____

Did your rap help you find or create new meaning to your story? Did your rap inspire others? How?

_____

_____

Ten Minutes of Dreaming

One of the best ways to achieve meaning in life is to plan for your future. This plan means creating measurable, achievable goals you can work toward. This exercise will provide you with the opportunity to dream. The best way to dream is without limitations. Do not put rules or guidelines on what you want to do in your future. For example, do not let your past, money, or other people's opinions determine what dreams you want to achieve. Instead, write down your dream below without any limits imposed on what you want to do.

Take the next ten minutes and answer the questions below.

What do you want your life to be like in the next five years? Please include where you want to live, where you want to work, what you want to spend your time on, who you want to be around, etc.

_____

_____

_____

_____

_____

_____

_____

_____

_____

_____

_____

_____

_____

_____

How did you feel when you wrote this?

_____

_____

_____

_____

_____

_____

_____

_____

Ten Minutes of Triumph

Your life will have additional meaning when you remember what a hero you are. Everyone is a hero in their own way. You have been a hero to people many times. For this activity, you will have the opportunity to give yourself a gold medal for something good that you did to help someone.

For example, perhaps you work in a helping profession where you were able to render aid to someone. Maybe you visited your neighbor who was grieving. Perhaps you were watching a friend's children while she was at school. Whatever heroic act you accomplished, it is time to congratulate yourself.

Take ten minutes to write down what you deserve a gold medal for in the lines below. Next, share it with a group or the facilitator so they can congratulate you on what you have done.

I, _____, am being awarded a gold medal for _____,

_____, and _____.

This event occurred on _____.

The character traits I exhibited included _____,

_____, _____, and _____.

What were the reactions of others when you told them how you were a hero?

_____

_____

_____

_____

_____

_____

_____

Ten Minutes of Advice to My Younger Self

Our greatest mistakes can become our greatest strengths because they add meaning to our lives and change our paths. No matter our age, we all have a younger self. This activity allows you to reflect on what you would like to tell your younger self. You can learn much about how you have grown and how your mistakes or successes have created meaning in your life. (Kristenson, 2022).

Take ten minutes and reflect on your younger self below.

What mistake created the greatest meaning for you?

_____

_____

_____

If you could go back in time five years and give your younger self advice, what would it be?

_____

_____

_____

If you could go back fifteen years and could tell your younger self anything, what would it be?

_____

_____

_____

If you went back in time and talked to your younger self, what would your younger self need?

_____

_____

_____

How did the choices of your younger self shape who you are today and the meaning in your life now?

_____

_____

_____

Ten Minutes of Taste

One of the best ways to create meaning is by using our senses. Our senses (taste, touch, smell, sight, and sound) help us survive and create emotions, memories, and meaning. Think of your favorite kind of grandma's cookies or a memorable family food tradition.

This activity will allow you to create meaning in ten minutes by tasting something delicious. A fascinating aspect of the brain is the amygdala, which attaches our emotions to memories and helps us develop good memories associated with taste. This process is a survival mechanism.

For the next ten minutes, list all the good memories you have associated with taste.

I like the taste of_____.

It means _____ to me.

———————— ◆ ❖ ◆ ————————

I like the taste of_____.

It means _____ to me.

———————— ◆ ❖ ◆ ————————

I like the taste of_____.

It means _____ to me.

———————— ◆ ❖ ◆ ————————

I like the taste of_____.

It means _____ to me.

———————— ◆ ❖ ◆ ————————

I like the taste of_____.

It means _____ to me.

Write down a list of the things you want to taste or try next and why (what this means to you).

_____

_____

_____

_____

Ten Minutes to the Olympics

Future goals add meaning to our lives. Sometimes it can be easy to forget that all larger goals (such as going to the Olympics) are initially broken down into smaller goals. This activity will allow you to choose a large goal and make a plan to work for the next 30 days on this goal for ten minutes each day.

Please follow the instructions below.

What is the larger goal you would like to achieve? Please describe the details of the goal below:

_____

_____

_____

_____

_____

For each day of the week below, please list what you will do for ten minutes each day to achieve this goal:

Sunday: _____

_____

Monday: _____

_____

Tuesday: _____

_____

Wednesday: _____

_____

Thursday: _____

_____

Friday: _____

_____

Saturday: _____

_____

Ten Minutes of Teaching

When we teach others, it adds meaning to our lives. For the next ten minutes, plan to teach someone something new. Everyone has something to teach. You have had different life experiences and know things others do not.

Think of a hobby, a talent, a skill, or information you would like to teach someone.

1. Pick one hobby, talent, or skill to teach others. *For example, beadwork, making necklaces, sewing, or making greeting cards.* Write it here.

    _____

    _____

2. Pick a person or group to whom you want to teach this skill. We all have skills to share with others. Who will you teach?

    _____

    _____

3. When will you teach this person or group your skill?

    _____

    _____

4. Why did you choose this person or group to teach your skill to? What does it mean to you to teach this person or group?

    _____

    _____

5. What did it mean to the person or group to have you teach them this skill?

    _____

    _____

The mediocre teacher tells. The good teacher explains.
The superior teacher demonstrates. The great teacher inspires.
~ William Arthur Ward

The Ten-Minute Autobiography

Everyone has a beautiful life story. We can create meaning for ourselves and others when we tell our story. Our past, present, and future are important because they all equal who we were, who we are, and who we will be. Specific events in our past have made us who we are, yet those events do not define us. We can choose to change, keeping pieces of our past that strengthen us. We can choose to let go of that which no longer serves us.

This activity allows you to spend ten minutes telling your life story to others. See what new meanings you derive from this ten-minute reflection period.

Give yourself ten minutes to reflect and share about your life. You can write on the back of this page or in a separate journal. Use the journaling prompts below for inspiration.

- ❖ Where and when were you born?

- ❖ What was your family like?

- ❖ Who was in your family?

- ❖ What was your personality growing up?

- ❖ Who was your biggest role model, and why?

- ❖ What was your biggest life decision, and why?

- ❖ Who has helped you the most, and why?

- ❖ What life experience has shaped you the most, and why?

- ❖ What is your favorite aspect of yourself, and why?

- ❖ Who is your favorite person, and why?

- ❖ What do you most look forward to, and why?

- ❖ What makes you laugh the most, and why?

Ten Minutes of Fame

There is a theoretical framework in psychology called acceptance and commitment therapy (ACT). One of the exercises in ACT is to have people picture what they want others to say about them and how they want to be remembered at the end of their life. This exercise helps people cope by creating more meaning. The qualities and values we live by motivate our actions and help us figure out who we want to become. Do you want to be remembered as a generous and giving person? If so, what are you doing now to be thought of as generous? Do you want to be remembered as helpful and smart?

List the qualities you want people to remember you by.

_____

_____

_____

_____

How are you living your life now to be remembered by the traits you have described above?

_____

_____

_____

_____

If you were to ask others to describe you, how would they do so now?

_____

_____

_____

_____

How has this exercise changed how you might live?

_____

_____

_____

_____

Level 1 Journaling

The following journaling prompts encourage personal self-discovery. *For each prompt, analyze central concepts of what you have learned by completing the therapeutic plan materials in this chapter.*

What is the first thing that comes to mind when you think of creating meaning in your life? Provide an example.

_____

_____

_____

_____

_____

_____

_____

What is your go-to task, hobby, or interest that creates meaning in your life?

_____

_____

_____

_____

_____

_____

_____

_____

Who has been the most influential in creating meaning in your life?

_____

_____

_____

_____

_____

_____

_____

_____

Level 2 Journaling

The following journaling prompts are reflective to help you develop metacognitive skills, increasing awareness of your learning processes by contemplating what you learned and how you learned it. *For each prompt, analyze central concepts of what you have learned by completing the therapeutic plan materials in this chapter.*

How can you add more positive colors to your wardrobe to be happier and more joyful?

_____

_____

_____

_____

_____

_____

_____

_____

Why is gratitude so critical in your life and the lives of others?

_____

_____

_____

_____

_____

_____

_____

_____

How does sharing your talents with others and service to others bring meaning into your life?

_____

_____

_____

_____

_____

_____

_____

_____

Level 3 Journaling

The following journaling prompts promote the development of wisdom by asking you to implement metacognitive skills in your daily life. ***For each prompt, analyze central concepts of what you have learned by completing the therapeutic plan materials in this chapter.***

What is the quickest way to create meaning in your life?

_____

_____

_____

_____

_____

_____

_____

_____

How will you proactively take steps to create meaning in your life today?

_____

_____

_____

_____

_____

_____

_____

_____

_____

What was the biggest turning point or lesson in your life that has created meaning for you?

_____

_____

_____

_____

_____

_____

_____

_____

—————————— **CHAPTER 2** ——————————

Make Meaning by Taking Action

Chapter 2 Therapeutic Plan

Goals
- Participants will learn how to create meaning by taking action.
- Participants will develop meaning in their lives by taking action in the following ways:
    1. Daily schedules
    2. Creating emergency preparation strategies
    3. Developing familiar routines
    4. Making connections with others
    5. Grounding themselves
- Participants will find meaning by:
    1. Learning something new
    2. Reflecting on their feelings
    3. Planning for the future
    4. Rituals
    5. Daily success

Actions
- Facilitators will explain and lead discussions about which activities will help participants create meaning in their lives.
- Facilitators should use each classroom, group situation, or one-on-one client session to structure and administer one or more worksheets to participants.
- Allow participants plenty of time to complete the worksheet.
- Participants can get into smaller groups or pairs to discuss their responses to the activities.
- At this time, participants can move into the larger group to provide opportunities to share their findings. Please remind all participants that they do not have to share anything they do not want to discuss. This space provides room for individuals to reflect; however, there is no obligation to do so.
- Individuals can share their self-discoveries with a trusted professional.

Demonstrations of Learning
- Journaling activities will help determine how much your participants have learned and if they have achieved their goals.
- Journaling activities at the end of each chapter should be given as homework assignments. Facilitators can administer the journaling activities near the beginning (Level 1 Journaling), in the middle (Level 2 Journaling), and near the end (Level 3 Journaling).
- As stated in the Introduction, facilitators can determine if and how to grade the journal entries.

Environment
- Move the seats into a large group, then break into smaller groups or pairs as necessary. When working with an individual client, create a comfortable, neutral environment.
- Download and print exercises from the workbook that are related to your specific topics.

Find Meaning Through Goals

One of the quickest ways to create meaning in your life is by creating and achieving goals. If goals are measurable, specific, and attainable, this will boost your mood substantially because your mind will have something to work toward.

Answer the following questions regarding the creation and attainment of your goals:

What is one goal you would like to attain this week?

_____

_____

_____

When will you attain this goal?

_____

_____

_____

How will you measure this goal?

_____

_____

_____

What action will you take today to reach this goal?

_____

_____

_____

How will the attainment of this goal create meaning for you this week or month?

_____

_____

_____

What goals do you have for the next year? What actions will you take today to achieve this?

_____

_____

_____

Meaning in Emergency Preparedness (Page 1)

While global or local emergencies are challenging, you can minimize the impact of emergencies by preparing ahead of time. There are numerous things you can do to take action and prepare for an emergency – both expected and unexpected.

This exercise will show you how taking action to prepare can mean a lot for you and your family during global change or any emergency. Doing big and small things to prepare ahead of time always helps.

Here are some tips for taking action to plan for emergencies. Place a checkmark in front of the ones that you already do.

- ☐ Have enough medication on hand in case you need to leave your home.

- ☐ Pack a go bag filled with emergency supplies such as personal items, medications, clothes, and important papers.

- ☐ Give your family members contact information about where they can reach you.

- ☐ Purchase enough flashlights and battery-powered lanterns in case of a power outage.

- ☐ Know where warm blankets, water, and nonperishable food supplies are stored.

- ☐ Learn about "home hardening" in preparation for wildfires. Purchase air purifiers to clean the air during fires.

- ☐ Have enough extra cash in case of emergency.

- ☐ Have a whistle, a dust mask, and a first aid kit.

- ☐ Have a hat, gloves, and warm clothes.

What is your plan of action for the items you have not checked?

_____

_____

_____

_____

_____

_____

(Continued on the next page)

Meaning in Emergency Preparedness (Page 2)

This exercise will allow you to reflect and make an action plan in preparation for natural disasters or an emergency. Preparing creates meaning in our lives because we can learn to value our health and safety. Psychologist Abraham Maslow described health and safety as "lower-level needs." He explained that survival needs like health and safety must be addressed before all other needs, such as socialization or achievement. Maslow created a hierarchy of needs, where lower-level needs (health and safety) must be satisfied before higher-level needs (such as self-actualization).

Please fill in the boxes below and explain how you plan to create meaning by taking action to prepare yourself and your family for an emergency.

Hierarchy of Needs	Actions You Will Take to Prepare
Physiological Needs for You and Your Family (Food, water, air, medications, medical supplies, and care)	
Safety Needs (To feel safe from injury or illness, as well as financial security)	
Belonging Needs (Having friends and family to support and care for each other)	
Esteem Needs (Feeling good about oneself)	
Self-Actualization Needs (Continuing work or school in a pandemic)	

Find Meaning in the Familiar (Page 1)

Often the most familiar and routine things bring the most meaning to our lives. They do not have to be large goals or something spectacular. The simplest things often mean the most. This exercise will help you find meaning in the most familiar circumstances.

To help you find meaning in the familiar, answer the following questions below:

What is the first thing you do every morning, and how does this help you start your day?

_____

_____

_____

Who do you see in person or talk to remotely daily that brings meaning to your life?

_____

_____

_____

What is one thing you can count on doing or happening every day, no matter what else is happening around you?

_____

_____

_____

What is it about your environment that makes you feel the most comfortable? What does this mean to you?

_____

_____

_____

Do you have a daily schedule? Describe it here. How does it help create meaning and hope for you?

_____

_____

_____

Often finding meaning is not about doing things differently;
it is about seeing familiar things in new ways.
~ Rachel Naomi Remen

(Continued on the next page)

Find Meaning in the Familiar (Page 2)

Familiar people, places, and routines bring us the greatest joy. Think of how good you feel to be home after a long vacation. Remember the times you have been greeted by an old friend and how comfortable you feel when you are together again.

Fill out the following worksheet so you can identify what feels most familiar to you and describe how it adds meaning to your life. Please note row one has space to write under each heading.

What Kinds of Things Are Familiar to You?	Why Do You Like It?	How Does This Add Meaning to Your Life?
Example: What kinds of things are familiar to you in the morning? *Taking your dog for a walk.*	*I like the exercise and enjoy chatting with my neighbor Sal.*	*I am able to get some exercise and watch the sunrise every morning. This puts me in a good mood.*
What Kinds of Things Are Familiar to You in the Morning?		
What Kinds of Things Are Familiar to You in the Afternoon?		
What Kinds of Things Are Familiar to You in the Evening?		
What Kinds of Things Are Familiar to You on the Weekends?		
What Is Most Familiar to You?		

Find Meaning in Connection

One of the best ways to find meaning is through connection with others. The people around us bring the most meaning to our lives. There are numerous ways to recognize and appreciate your connections, expand your social networks, increase your connections, and enhance your sense of purpose.

Put a check next to the ways you find meaning through connection with others.

- ☐ **Communicating with my co-workers**
- ☐ **Being with my family**
- ☐ **Spending time with my children**
- ☐ **Volunteer work for others**
- ☐ **A phone call to an old friend**
- ☐ **My connection to my medical providers**
- ☐ **My relationships with my neighbors**
- ☐ **Connect with cashiers, bank tellers, and coffee baristas (familiar strangers)**
- ☐ **Relationship with my spouse, partner, or significant other**
- ☐ **On-line communications with others**
- ☐ **Playing a sport and being part of a team**
- ☐ **Engaging in a hobby that involves a connection with others (art classes)**
- ☐ **Traveling and meeting new people**

Of the ways to connect above, which is your favorite way to create meaning? Why?

_____

_____

_____

Which type of connection above would you like to incorporate more of? Why?

_____

_____

_____

Find Meaning While Meeting New People

One of the best parts about traveling is meeting new people. It creates more meaning because we learn to value the opinions, languages, and cultures of others. You can take action today to start meeting new people. The more we are exposed to new cultures and ideas, the richer and more meaningful our lives will become. Below are some ideas to get you started meeting new people so you can bring more joy and meaning into your life. Reflect on the suggestions provided, then fill the other boxes with your ideas.

There are many ways to meet people.

Say hello to a stranger on a walk	Ask someone for help	Invite someone out for coffee or a meal	Congratulate people	Smile at someone	Introduce yourself to someone
Get to know someone sitting next to you on a plane ride	Sign up to take a class	Compliment people	Volunteer for a non-profit organization		

How has meeting new people added meaning to your life?

_____

_____

_____

Find Meaning in Rituals

Rituals often bring us joy and meaning. They are similar to routines, a series of actions done the same way each time. Rituals are often traditions based on various views, cultures, social networks, and history. They include gatherings with family and friends for cultural events, graduations, weddings, births, deaths, holidays, and ceremonies.

Please fill in the blanks with your rituals and how they create meaning in your life.

Ritual	Dates and Times	People, places, and things involved	Meaning in Your Life
Example: Annual picnic at the lake.	*First Sunday in August.*	*Picnic with neighbors.*	*Seeing important people every year.*

Which ritual brings you the most meaning?

_____

_____

_____

Find Meaning from Hope

Hope creates joy and meaning in our lives. When we have hope, we have optimism about the future. Anything you can do to start planning for the future (even something in the next ten minutes) can help you create instant meaning and increase your happiness. You can create meaning and hope by planning both big and small things. For example, having chocolate in ten minutes, or planning a trip to Hawaii next fall, can improve your mood and hope rapidly.

Please circle anything from the list below that you are looking forward to and that creates meaning in your life:

Going to the beach	**Finishing a work project**
Taking a walk	**Playing a sport**
Having coffee with a friend	**Engaging in a hobby**
Cooking your favorite meal	**Going out to dinner**
Watching your favorite TV show	**Watching your favorite movie**
Talking with co-workers	**Planning next year's vacation**
Petting your pet	**Listening to your favorite song**
Attending your favorite class	**Reading a book**

Now you add some that are not listed:

Others:

_____

_____

_____

_____

What do you notice about the activities you circled or listed?

_____

_____

_____

_____

Create Meaning by Grounding

Children's brains develop at rocket speed. Everything is new and different to a child. Stimuli are continuously being presented to kids. Life can have new meaning if we learn to see with children's eyes and marvel at the beauty around us, seeing things from a fresh perspective. One of the ways to create meaning and see things in a new and exciting way is through mindful grounding exercises, finding meaning through your senses: sight, sound, touch, taste, and smell.

Take some time to create meaning by completing the grounding exercises below. When you complete each exercise, write a paragraph on a separate sheet of paper about how the exercise created meaning for you.

1. Take a mindful walk to ground yourself. When you are on your walk, count how many steps you take. When your mind wanders elsewhere, return to counting your steps.

2. Take a new route on your regular commute or drive. Notice what new things you see when you drive in a different direction.

3. Have a delicious meal. Notice the taste of the food on your tongue and how this makes you feel. Take your time eating each item of food.

4. Feel something warm and cozy, like a soft pillow or blanket. Notice how you feel when your hands touch this material.

5. Look out your window and notice something new (a flower, a tree, or a bird).

6. Watch the sunset.

7. Listen for a sound around you. Pick a sound to focus on. Close your eyes and focus only on that sound.

Describe the new meaning you found when you engaged in the exercises above. How did they help you see things in a new light?

_____

_____

_____

_____

_____

_____

_____

_____

_____

Create Meaning Out of Challenges

Sometimes our greatest challenges become our greatest strengths. This exercise will help you reflect on how your difficulties can be redefined to help you grow. This reflection is a skill that takes practice. We can turn any problem into a solution by redefining it.

Complete the activity below by describing how to create new meaning from a problem.

1. Take a few moments to describe a current or past problem. *For example, my elderly cat died, and I secluded myself in my grief.*

_____

_____

_____

_____

_____

2. Explain how you could overcome the problem by creating new meaning. *I could start volunteering at animal shelters where I'm helping others and have compassionate company in my sadness.*

_____

_____

_____

_____

_____

3. What steps did you take to redefine this problem? What new thoughts did you use to create new meaning?

_____

_____

_____

_____

_____

No act of kindness, no matter how small, is ever wasted.
~ Aesop

Create Meaning by Learning Something New

We find meaning by expanding our knowledge or skills. Create meaning by learning a new hobby, skill, trade, or anything that will expand your mind.

This exercise will help you discover creative avenues to learn new things. Please choose something new to learn (either from the list below or picking something new yourself).

Start with these reflection questions.

1. What is something you have always wanted to learn?

    _____

    _____

    _____

2. What would it mean for your life if you learned it?

    _____

    _____

    _____

3. What has stopped you in the past from learning this new thing?

    _____

    _____

    _____

4. Commit to learning it. How will you do this?

    _____

    _____

    _____

5. How will this change your life?

    _____

    _____

    _____

6. Who will help you learn this?

    _____

    _____

    _____

Create Meaning Through a Hierarchy of Hope (Page 1)

You can make new meaning if you have hopefulness. You can create hope in a variety of ways. One of the models that can help you is the Hierarchy of Hope. This theory explains that hope can be created during a difficult time when you focus on your future goals and your higher and lower-level needs.

The Hierarchy of Hope model posits that individuals can develop a sense of meaning after a difficulty, trauma, or pivot point that motivates them to change directions. There are several stages to the Hierarchy of Hope theory, including the following: **meaning, accomplishment, relationships, control, and engagement**.

For each section, comment on how you will gain hope through the journaling questions below. These questions will help you begin to develop hope in the midst of global change or other life events.

Meaning: How can you begin to make a meaningful contribution to the world?

_____

_____

_____

What does this mean for your life?

_____

_____

_____

◆ ❖ ◆

Accomplishment: How can you begin to feel good about yourself? How can you begin preparing for additional future successes?

_____

_____

_____

What does this mean for your life?

_____

_____

_____

(Continued on the next page)

Create Meaning Through a Hierarchy of Hope (Page 2)

Relationships: How have your relationships changed? How can you develop additional meaningful, hopeful relationships?

_____

_____

_____

What does this mean for your life?

_____

_____

_____

◆ ❖ ◆

Control: How have you lost a sense of control in life? How can you regain this control so that you are more hopeful? You can maintain hope by changing the meaning of your circumstances and living in a new way.

_____

_____

_____

What does this mean for your life?

_____

_____

_____

◆ ❖ ◆

Engagement: How have you become less engaged in life? How can you become more engaged? How can you develop or rediscover skills and talents leading to a path of hope?

_____

_____

_____

What does this mean for your life?

_____

_____

_____

Level 1 Journaling

The following journaling prompts encourage personal self-discovery. ***For each prompt, analyze central concepts of what you have learned by completing the therapeutic plan materials in this chapter.***

What familiar people, places, and things bring you the most joy?

_____

_____

_____

_____

_____

_____

_____

What parts of your daily routine are your favorite? *For example, your morning coffee, your quiet walk with your dog, or waking up your child before school.*

_____

_____

_____

_____

_____

_____

_____

What parts of your roots bring you the most joy?

_____

_____

_____

_____

_____

_____

_____

Level 2 Journaling

The following journaling prompts are reflective to help you develop metacognitive skills, increasing awareness of your learning processes by contemplating what you learned and how you learned it. *For each prompt, analyze central concepts of what you have learned by completing the therapeutic plan materials in this chapter.*

What has created the most meaning in your life?

_____

_____

_____

_____

_____

_____

_____

How has taking action been a catalyst for helping you create meaning?

_____

_____

_____

_____

_____

_____

_____

What is one way you plan to take more action starting today?

_____

_____

_____

_____

_____

_____

_____

Level 3 Journaling

The following journaling prompts promote the development of wisdom by asking you to implement metacognitive skills in your daily life. *For each prompt, analyze central concepts of what you have learned by completing the therapeutic plan materials in this chapter.*

Who has inspired you to take action?

_____

_____

_____

_____

_____

_____

_____

What has been the biggest turning point in your life?

_____

_____

_____

_____

_____

_____

_____

What was the biggest turning point or lesson that has created meaning for you?

_____

_____

_____

_____

_____

_____

_____

—————————— **CHAPTER 3** ——————————

Discover Meaning Through Mental Health Fitness

Chapter 3 Therapeutic Plan

Goals

- Participants will learn how to create meaning by examining their mental health.
- Participants will develop meaning in their lives by utilizing tools that help address their mental health needs each day.
- Participants will find meaning by using techniques such as:
    1. Radically accepting their feelings
    2. Exercising their mental health muscles
    3. Making mental health magic
    4. Feeling good
    5. Reaching out to others to share

Actions

- Facilitators will explain and lead discussions about which activities help them create meaning in their lives.
- Facilitators should use each classroom, group situation, or one-on-one client session to structure and administer one or more worksheets to participants.
- Allow participants plenty of time to complete the worksheet.
- Participants can get into smaller groups or pairs to discuss their responses to the activities.
- At this time, participants can move into the larger group to provide opportunities to share their findings. Please remind all participants that they do not have to share anything they do not want to discuss. This space provides room for individuals to reflect; however, there is no obligation to do so.
- Individuals can share their self-discoveries with a trusted professional.

Demonstrations of Learning

- Journaling activities will help determine how much your participants have learned and if they have achieved their goals.
- Journaling activities at the end of each chapter should be given as homework assignments. Facilitators can administer the journaling activities near the beginning (Level 1 Journaling), in the middle (Level 2 Journaling), and near the end (Level 3 Journaling).
- As stated in the Introduction, facilitators can determine if and how to grade the journal entries.

Environment

- Move the seats into a large group, then break into smaller groups or pairs as necessary. When working with an individual client, create a comfortable, neutral environment.
- Download and print exercises from the workbook that are related to your specific topics.

Find Meaning by Staying Mentally Fit

Just as it is important to maintain our physical fitness, it is also crucial to take care of our mental fitness. We all have a mental health status. The term mental health applies to everyone, regardless of their emotional state. Some people walk, others lift weights, and others may look for a balanced diet to maintain their physical health. ***Describe the ways you maintain your mental and physical fitness in each category below.***

How do you stay in tune with your feelings every day?

Please describe how you stay in tune with your feelings each day. *For example, you might talk to a friend, listen to music that expresses your feelings, or use a feelings wheel.*

_____

_____

_____

How do you express yourself every day?

Please describe how you express yourself each day. *For example, you might have one person you check in with every morning or a website you visit regularly. You might journal your feelings every night.*

_____

_____

_____

What are your little things?

Everyone has little things that help them feel better. What small things do you do each day to help yourself remain stable and feel better? *For example, maybe you go for a walk and breathe fresh air in the morning or get your favorite warm drink.*

_____

_____

_____

Who, what, and where is your support?

We survive because of relationships. Where and from whom do you feel the most supported? *For example, maybe you are connected to a PTA group or involved in a neighborhood baseball team.*

_____

_____

_____

Find Meaning by Getting to Know Yourself

The better we know ourselves, the more meaning our lives will have. When we understand the meanings behind our experiences, we understand ourselves, others, and the world a little bit better. We find meaning through life experiences and the emotions we attach to these situations. In fact, it is our emotions that bring us the most meaning.

This exercise will help you find meaning in a current life circumstance by examining your past and present feelings. Please follow the directions in the journaling prompts below:

Describe a current life circumstance. *For example, "I am upset about not getting the promotion at work."*

_____

_____

_____

_____

Describe the feelings you have about the current situation. *For example, "I feel sad now."*

_____

_____

_____

_____

Think of a time in the past when you had feelings similar to the situation you described above. *For example, "I felt sad in the past in junior high."*

_____

_____

_____

_____

Describe your past experience. *For example, "I was sad when I did not make the junior high baseball all-star team."*

_____

_____

_____

_____

Find Meaning by Feeling Good

You can find meaning in numerous ways by proactively searching for ways to feel good. When we have enjoyable experiences and feel happy, this creates good memories. Our brain automatically wants to repeat the things that help us feel better. Think of a fun vacation with friends that made you feel good and that you want to do all over again. This situation created a positive meaning for you. The associations our brains make with positive situations make us feel good so we can have more meaning in our lives.

This activity will help you work on creating positive associations. You can learn to feel good and find meaning in your life. The more positive associations you make, the more meaning you will have.

Begin this activity by listing the things that make you feel good, why these things make you feel good, and the positive associations or memories you have with these things.

One of my top feel-good activities is:
Example: Walking with a friend.

_____

_____

Why does this make me feel good?
Example: I like to share stories and feelings with my friend and get exercise.

_____

_____

What are my positive associations with this activity?
Example: I associate walking and my friend with positive emotions like joy, laughter, and happiness.

_____

_____

◆ ❖ ◆

One of my top feel-good activities is:

_____

_____

Why does this make me feel good?

_____

_____

What are my positive associations with this activity?

_____

_____

Find Meaning by Finding Yourself

The better we know ourselves, the more meaning we have. When we understand what brings us comfort, joy, happiness, and change, we have the knowledge to live a good life. Our past creates a lens through which we interpret and make sense of our current experiences.

This exercise will help you understand the meaning of your current emotions based on your past experiences. The past, present, and future make up who you are. ***Complete the journaling prompts below.***

Describe in detail a current or recent situation when you had strong feelings.

_____

_____

_____

_____

What are your feelings (sad, mad, glad, scared, or others)?

_____

_____

_____

_____

Describe in detail a situation in your past (remote or recent) when you remember having similar feelings to those you have today. What were your feelings that were the same (sad, mad, glad, scared, or others)?

_____

_____

_____

_____

What did you learn in this exercise about the meaning you have attached to the current situation? What did you learn about the meaning of your emotions?

_____

_____

_____

_____

Find Meaning Through Radical Acceptance

We may suffer most from our feelings when we have difficulties accepting what is. Rather than trying to stop our feelings and experiences, we can radically accept our situation, which frees us to make necessary life changes and create new meaning. Dr. Linehan, a psychologist, utilized radical acceptance to help clients find peace as they struggled with their emotions. (Linehan, 2014)

This exercise is designed to help you create new meaning by radically accepting your situation. Radical acceptance is a great coping skill and an excellent way to find meaning through difficult circumstances.

Please draw or describe one current situation you are having trouble accepting or wish was different.

Please draw or describe what would be different if you completely accept what is happening or what has happened and how you might feel different.

Make Meaning with a Mental Health Day

Just as important as planning vacations, planning a mental health day is crucial. A mental health day can mean different things to different people. For some people, a mental health day may mean taking time to go to a therapy appointment. For others, it might mean taking the day off from all other activities and working on self-care.

Everyone needs time to take care of themselves. There are no rules for a mental health day. A mental health day is a way to recharge your mind, body, and soul. When you take a mental health day, you are valuing your own needs, so you have greater capacity to give to the world.

Here are some ideas of things you can do on a mental health day:

❖ Take a long hike outside and breathe in the fresh air.

❖ Go to see your therapist.

❖ Meet a friend you have not seen for a long time.

❖ Go to a movie and laugh hard.

❖ Cook or order your favorite meal.

❖ Plan your next vacation.

❖ Sip tea and write in your journal.

❖ Go shopping and buy a new outfit.

❖ Go to a sporting event.

❖ Take a long drive and listen to your favorite music.

❖ Clean your house.

❖ Add in your ideas: _____

❖ Add in your ideas: _____

❖ Add in your ideas: _____

Make Meaning with Daily Mantras

Mantras are positive affirmations you can repeat to yourself. They are designed to help you feel good about yourself and raise your self-esteem. You can say mantras to yourself, or you can post them on your computer, your door, your mirror, or your cereal box.

Think of a few mantras or positive quotes you can tell yourself often. Thinks of creative places where you can write them down and read them. Pick quotes or mantras that mean something to you.

Here are some examples of mantras:

I am a valuable human being.

All of my needs are important.

I am capable and talented.

I can do it.

Which mantras do you want to tell yourself, and where will you post them?

1. _____

2. _____

3. _____

Examples of positive quotes include:

If you see someone without a smile today, give 'em yours.
~ Dolly Parton

People begin to become successful the minute they decide to be.
~ Harvey McKay

What are your favorite quotes, and what creative places will you find to post them?

1. _____

2. _____

3. _____

Find Meaning with Friends

Spending time with friends is a great way to create meaning in your life. Your time together can be in person, on a virtual platform, through writing letters, or on the phone. Making memories with friends is one of the most meaningful parts of life. The meaning you derive from friendships can be in the past, present, or future. You can remember the good times, the times your friends helped you, and the times you had fun.

Past - Please describe your best memories with friends and explain what this means to you. Explain how you added meaning to their lives too.

Present - Please describe what your current friends are like and how they help you. Describe what your closest friends mean to you. Describe how you help your friends, too.

Future - Please describe what type of support you anticipate needing in the future from friends. Describe what this will mean to your future self?

**Making plans for the future is an important way to create meaning and hope.
Planning your next trip to see friends is good for your soul.**

Find Meaning with Mental Health Magic (Page 1)

A long time ago, there was a magician that roamed the countryside granting wishes. He would approach people and tell them that he would grant them one wish if they could describe how their life would be different, and how they could help other people as a result of the wish being granted.

List one wish (in as much detail as possible) for your life:

_____

_____

_____

_____

_____

_____

How would your life be different today if your wish was granted?

_____

_____

_____

_____

_____

_____

_____

What steps could you take to ensure you reach this wished-for future?

_____

_____

_____

_____

_____

_____

_____

(Continued on the next page)

Find Meaning with Mental Health Magic (Page 2)

Now that you have had your wish granted, it is time to help other people. Helping people provides meaning in life. How could you find ways to help others improve their lives while making your life more meaningful? *In each of the spaces that follow, draw some of the people, animals, or situations you might like to help. Then write about how you will begin helping them.*

People, Animals, Situations I Want to Help…	People, Animals, Situations I Want to Help…
How I Will Help:	How I Will Help:
People, Animals, Situations I Want to Help…	People, Animals, Situations I Want to Help…
How I Will Help:	How I Will Help:

Make Meaning with Mental Health Success

Solution-focused therapy (De Shazer et al., 1986) helps people imagine their lives without problems and encourages them to find ways to live as if their problems are already solved. Start challenging yourself to live in a new way by assuming you will succeed.

Please answer the following dare questions to help yourself live your best life.

What would you do today if you knew you could not fail?

_____

_____

_____

_____

_____

_____

_____

What would you do differently today if you knew you would succeed?

_____

_____

_____

_____

_____

_____

_____

How would your relationships be different if you knew you would succeed? How would your actions be different?

_____

_____

_____

_____

_____

_____

_____

Find Meaning with a Mental Health Therapist

Just as it is important to discuss your physical health with a medical provider, paying attention to your mental health is also crucial. A mental health therapist helps you feel better in many ways. You do not need to wait to see a therapist until you are in great distress; however, if you are feeling very depressed, please contact a therapist or call emergency services immediately (such as 911).

Here are some ways a mental health therapist can help you:

1. A therapist is a neutral person who can listen to your problems without judgment.

2. A therapist can help you understand why you feel the way you do.

3. A therapist can help you cope with global changes.

4. A therapist can help you process your thoughts, feelings, and actions.

5. A therapist can help you make the necessary changes to have the life you want.

6. A therapist can help you develop goals so you can become more hopeful.

7. A therapist can help you through life transitions (moves, job changes, relationship changes, etc.)

8. A therapist can help you with important life decisions.

What are some of the things you could use support with?

1._____

2._____

3._____

4._____

5._____

6._____

There is easier access to mental health resources today than ever before. Seeking mental health support has become less stigmatized.

If you need help accessing mental health, check with your local community resource centers, insurance provider, primary care provider, local school districts, or call 911 for assistance.

Make Meaning with Your Mental Health Muscles

Just as we need to exercise our bodies, it is important to strengthen our mental health muscles. We can strengthen our mental health muscles by practicing ways to cope, relax, and feel better.

Cope – You can find new ways to cope with difficulties, such as walking, journaling your feelings, and talking to someone who will listen. You can create a plan for yourself. How do you cope? *For example, if you are upset, does taking a long drive help your mood?*

_____

_____

_____

Think – How can you change your thoughts to feel better? *For example, instead of thinking, "This test is hard," try thinking, "I can do this."*

_____

_____

_____

Act – Do you notice you act differently when you are in different moods? *For example, do you listen better to others when you are more relaxed?*

_____

_____

_____

Seek Support – Do you feel better when you give and receive enough emotional support? Who is your support system? *For example, "I get together with Clara when I need to talk."*

_____

_____

_____

Have Fun – Everyone's mood improves when they have a good time. *For example, you feel better when you spend time with someone laughing.* How do you have fun?

_____

_____

_____

Relax – Our bodies need time to rest and recharge when we are busy and experiencing change or stress. *For example, when you take time to close your eyes and breathe deeply, you may feel better.* How do you relax?

_____

_____

_____

Make Meaning by Writing Your Own Movie

One of the best ways to understand your life is to write your life story as if it were a movie or a show. This exercise will help you find meaning in your life by illustrating your own story. ***Create an outline for your life movie below. Start with a beginning, a middle with a turning point, change, or lesson, and a current-day description of the lessons you learned or are continuing to learn.***

Beginning of your movie. Start with your childhood, where you grew up, who your family was, what your life was like etc.

_____

_____

_____

_____

_____

Middle of your movie. The changes you have experienced and the turning point of your life.

_____

_____

_____

_____

_____

Current day meaning. The lessons you have learned that changed your life. What you will continue to strive for in the future.

_____

_____

_____

_____

_____

What did you learn by writing down the script of your life?

_____

_____

_____

_____

_____

Level 1 Journaling

The following journaling prompts encourage personal self-discovery. ***For each prompt, analyze central concepts of what you have learned by completing the therapeutic plan materials in this chapter.***

What does staying mentally fit mean to you?

_____

_____

_____

_____

_____

_____

_____

_____

Who, what, when, and where keeps you mentally fit?

_____

_____

_____

_____

_____

_____

_____

_____

How would you describe the meaning of your mental health fitness to someone you just met?

_____

_____

_____

_____

_____

_____

_____

_____

Level 2 Journaling

The following journaling prompts are reflective to help you develop metacognitive skills, increasing awareness of your learning processes by contemplating what you learned and how you learned it. ***For each prompt, analyze central concepts of what you have learned by completing the therapeutic plan materials in this chapter.***

How does getting to know yourself help you create new meaning?

_____

_____

_____

_____

_____

_____

_____

_____

How does radically accepting your circumstances help you change?

_____

_____

_____

_____

_____

_____

_____

_____

What happens when you accept your emotions?

_____

_____

_____

_____

_____

_____

_____

Level 3 Journaling

The following journaling prompts promote the development of wisdom by asking you to implement metacognitive skills in your daily life. ***For each prompt, analyze central concepts of what you have learned by completing the therapeutic plan materials in this chapter.***

What is your current mental health status, and how does this knowledge help you?

_____

_____

_____

_____

_____

_____

_____

_____

What was the best day of your life, and what did this mean?

_____

_____

_____

_____

_____

_____

_____

_____

What are your favorite people, places, and things? What do these mean to you?

_____

_____

_____

_____

_____

_____

_____

_____

CHAPTER 4

Meaning Through Establishing Self-Worth

Chapter 4 Therapeutic Plan

Goals
- Participants will learn about the concept of self-worth.
- Participants will be able to identify the connection between self-worth and meaning in life.
- Participants will learn how to engage in healthy, meaningful activities that enhance their feelings of self-worth.

Actions
- Facilitators will explain and lead discussions about the importance of self-worth in helping people live their lives to the fullest.
- Facilitators should use each classroom, group situation, or one-on-one client session to structure and administer one or more worksheets to participants.
- Allow participants plenty of time to complete the worksheet.
- Participants can get into smaller groups or pairs to discuss their responses to the activities.
- At this time, participants can move into the larger group to provide opportunities to share their findings. Please remind all participants that they do not have to share anything they do not want to discuss. This space provides room for individuals to reflect; however, there is no obligation to do so.
- Individuals can share their self-discoveries with a trusted professional.

Demonstrations of Learning
- Journaling activities will help determine how much your participants have learned and if they have achieved their goals.
- Journaling activities at the end of each chapter should be given as homework assignments. Facilitators can administer the journaling activities near the beginning (Level 1 Journaling), in the middle (Level 2 Journaling), and near the end (Level 3 Journaling).
- As stated in the Introduction, facilitators can determine if and how to grade the journal entries.

Environment
- Move the seats into a large group, then break into smaller groups or pairs as necessary. When working with an individual client, create a comfortable, neutral environment.
- Download and print exercises from the workbook that are related to your specific topics.

Self-Awareness Scale (Page 1)

Name _____ Date _____

It is essential to be aware of the many aspects of yourself to live a meaningful life.

Look at the items that follow to gauge your self-awareness. In each statement, circle YES if the statement applies to you and NO if it does not.

I understand the emotions I feel in my body _____ YES _____ NO

I successfully express my feelings _____ YES _____ NO

I rarely distract myself to avoid feeling my emotions_____ YES _____ NO

I talk to others about my feelings _____ YES _____ NO

I am aware of my feelings as I feel them _____ YES _____ NO

My Feelings TOTAL _____

I listen to my inner voice rather than being influenced by others _____ YES _____ NO

I know who I really am deep inside _____ YES _____ NO

I understand and live by my values_____ YES _____ NO

I understand my worth as a human being _____ YES _____ NO

I believe that I have self-worth exactly as I am _____ YES _____ NO

Self-Awareness TOTAL _____

I feel good about myself most days _____ YES _____ NO

I take responsibility for my actions _____ YES _____ NO

I feel like I'm a worthy person _____ YES _____ NO

I feel like I'm living my true purpose in life _____ YES _____ NO

I have immense respect for myself _____ YES _____ NO

Self-Esteem TOTAL _____

I get enough sleep to function well _____ YES _____ NO

I have a regular exercise routine _____ YES _____ NO

I regularly eat healthy, nutritious foods _____ YES _____ NO

I am assertive and say no when I need to _____ YES _____ NO

I unplug from technology when I need to _____ YES _____ NO

Self-Care TOTAL _____

(Continued on the next page)

Self-Awareness Scale (Page 2)

Scoring Directions

Count the YES answers you circled and put that number on the Total line beneath each section. Then, transfer your totals to the spaces below:

My Feelings   Total = _____

Self-Awareness   Total = _____

Self-Esteem   Total = _____

Self-Care   Total = _____

Profile Interpretation

Scores (the number of YES answers you circled) on the assessment range from 0 to 5. The higher your score, the more self-aware you tend to be. ***Look at the descriptions for each of the scales below and answer the journaling prompt.***

Scale Descriptions

My Feelings – People scoring high on this scale understand the emotions generated in their bodies, understand the feelings associated with these emotions, and express their feelings in constructive ways.
- How can you get more in touch with your emotions and the subsequent feelings?

Self-Awareness – People scoring high on this scale tend to be self-aware. They understand and live by their values, know who they are, and have self-worth just as they are.
- How can you understand your values, uniqueness, and gifts more?

Self-Esteem – People scoring high on this scale feel good about themselves and their lives. They respect themselves and believe they are living their true purpose.
- What changes do you need to make to feel better about yourself?

Self-Care – People scoring high on this scale take great care of themselves by eating nutritious food, exercising, and getting adequate sleep.
- What changes can you make to take better care of yourself?

Self-awareness is the ability to take an honest look at your life without any attachment to it being right or wrong, good or bad.
~ Debbie Ford

My Strengths

All people have strengths and weaknesses. People often focus only on their weaknesses. It's important to be aware of your strengths so that you can use them to make meaning in your life. When you understand your strengths, you can use them to make meaning by engaging in activities that accentuate them. Strengths include work skills, spare-time interests, family obligations, community activities, and personality characteristics.

Write about your strengths below.

My Strength	How I Can Use This Strength	How This Strength is a Positive in My Life	How It Adds Meaning to My Life
Example: I enjoy working with older adults.	*I will see if the senior center in my neighborhood needs someone to engage in activities with its residents.*	*I really enjoy giving back to people who have dedicated their lives to raising kids and helping younger people.*	*Helping others makes my life fulfilling. I feel like I am adding to the greater good of society.*

Self-awareness is not self-centeredness, and spirituality is not narcissism. "Know thyself" is not a narcissistic pursuit.
~ Marianne Williamson

I am Unique

Uniqueness – The qualities of being the only one of its kind, particularly remarkable, special, or unusual.

Your uniqueness adds meaning to your life. For example, you may be an excellent communicator, which adds value and meaning through clear communication with family members and friends to avoid misunderstandings.

Think about how you are unique and how your uniqueness adds value and meaning to your life. Then, complete the sentence starters that follow.

I am unique because…

_____

_____

This uniqueness adds value and meaning to my life by…

_____

_____

◆ ❖ ◆

I am unique because…

_____

_____

This uniqueness adds value and meaning to my life by…

_____

_____

◆ ❖ ◆

I am unique because…

_____

_____

This uniqueness adds value and meaning to my life by…

_____

_____

Who Am I?

One of the biggest questions all people have to answer is, "Who Am I?" The answer to this question relates to how you will find meaning in your life.

In the spaces that follow, draw, doodle, or write about who you think you are. For personality attributes, you might draw a picture of someone who is outgoing and talking to people.

Personality Attributes	Values
How They Will Help Me Find Meaning:	How They Will Help Me Find Meaning:

Talents/Skills	Interests
How They Will Help Me Find Meaning:	How They Will Help Me Find Meaning:

Why Am I Here?

A crucial aspect of finding your sense of meaning and purpose is determining "Why am I on this earth?" When you can answer this question, you will be on your way to discovering your true purpose in life. Please remember that through purpose comes meaning.

Answer the following sentence starters to begin narrowing down aspects related to your sense of purpose.

I believe that I am here to…

_____

_____

I think my most important talent, skill, or gift is…

_____

_____

I can use this talent, skill, or gift to help humanity by…

_____

_____

My meaningful life's work is…

_____

_____

I would describe my character, including my virtues, vices, strengths, and weaknesses, as…

_____

_____

The things that bring me joy include…

_____

_____

The one thing I want to do with my life is…

_____

_____

Longitudinal Narrative

An effective way to create more meaning in your life is to examine the stories from your past, present, and anticipated future related to who you are. ***For each of the three boxes, examine a story that describes meaning and purpose in your life.*** *For example, my grandmother came directly from Czechoslovakia and told me many stories of her life in the old country. I have been fascinated with traveling and seeing different cultures ever since. I will visit the Czech Republic next year, and in the future, I hope to host students from that country.*

My Story About the Past

My Story About the Present

My Story About the Future

Who are we but the stories we tell ourselves, about ourselves, and believe?
~ Scott Turow

Quotations: Agree or Disagree?

Self-awareness means different things to different people. With which of the following quotes do you most agree? With which do you most disagree?

Life is really not easy, we all have our personal battles, but it is important that you really treasure yourself, love yourself, and have a sense of self-worth.
~ Heart Evangelista

Do you agree or disagree? Why?

_____

_____

Your self-worth has nothing to do with your craft or calling, and everything to do with how you treat yourself.
~ Kris Carr

Do you agree or disagree? Why?

_____

_____

Only when you are aware of the uniqueness of everyone's individual body will you begin to have a sense of your own self-worth.
~ Ma Jian

Do you agree or disagree? Why?

_____

_____

The best way to avoid falling prey to the opinions of others is to realize that other people's opinions are just that - opinions. Regardless of how great or terrible they think you are, that's only their opinion. Your true self-worth comes from within.
~ Travis Bradberry

Do you agree or disagree? Why?

_____

_____

My Heroes

Your heroes are those people you admire or idealize. They could be alive, dead, historical, or fictional. Who are two of your heroes?

Draw pictures or use single words that depict two of your heroes below:

Hero #1	Hero #2

Name three meaningful qualities or values that Hero #1 possesses.

_____

_____

_____

How do these meaningful qualities or values provide you with meaning in your life?

_____

_____

_____

Name any admirable qualities you have that are the same as this hero.

_____

_____

_____

Name three meaningful qualities or values that Hero #2 possesses.

_____

_____

_____

How do these meaningful qualities or values provide you with meaning in your life?

_____

_____

_____

Name any admirable qualities you have that are the same as this hero.

_____

_____

_____

I'm a More Positive Thinker

Your self-worth is related to the thoughts you have about yourself. Your level of self-worth depends on how positively you see yourself and the stream-of-conscious thoughts that constantly invade your thinking. To ensure that you have constant positive thoughts in your head, you can use the following formula to help you:

Phase 1: Monitor the thoughts as you think them. For example, "I should be as wealthy as they are."

Phase 2: Note the feelings prompted by the negative thought. Become more aware of the feelings (sadness, insecurity, jealousy, etc.) triggered by the negative thought.

Phase 3: Work to reverse the effect of the thought so that it is more optimistic. You could alter the negative thought so that it is positive and does not trigger any negative emotions. For example, "I have enough money to satisfy my needs" and "Money doesn't buy happiness."

Use the following three-step process to turn some of your less-than-positive thoughts into very positive thoughts.

Phase 1: Monitor the thoughts as you think them.

_____

_____

Phase 2: Note the feelings prompted by the negative thought.

_____

_____

Phase 3: Work to reverse the effect of the thought so that it is more optimistic.

_____

_____

◆ ❖ ◆

Phase 1: Monitor the thoughts as you think them.

_____

_____

Phase 2: Note the feelings prompted by the negative thought.

_____

_____

Phase 3: Work to reverse the effect of the thought so that it is more optimistic.

_____

_____

Find Like-Minded People

To have more meaning in your life, you can connect with people you share interests with by participating in community activities. What social activities are offered in your community, local schools or universities, houses of worship, fitness centers, or clubs that you might enjoy?

Possible Connections	Why I Might Like It	How I Can Get Involved
Example: I can meet new people at a martials arts class.	*I'll get exercise, learn to defend myself, and meet people with similar interests.*	*I'll look online and visit the martial arts studios near me.*

For one of the options you listed above, set a long-term goal and a few short-term goals to make it happen.

Long-term goal: _____

_____

Short-term goals: _____

_____

Grounded Breathing Practice

Grounded breathing is much more than simply the movement of air in and out of your lungs. It is a practice that enhances your bodily functions and increases your life force. Practicing this type of breathing can relax your mind, calm your emotions, enhance your self-awareness, and explore your purpose.

Practice Grounded Breathing:

1. Find a quiet place to practice. Sit quietly in a meditative posture, allowing each breath to get longer and deeper. It might help you to count your breaths. To do so, begin by breathing in for the count of three, retain the breath for a count of three, release the air to the count of three, and then rest upon exhaling to a count of three. Continue this practice for several cycles.

   What were your reactions?

   _____

   _____

   _____

   _____

2. Slowly increase the count of three for inhaling, retaining the breath, releasing the air, and resting upon exhaling.

   How does it feel?

   _____

   _____

   _____

   _____

3. As you breathe, reflect on the question, "What is my purpose in life?"

   What did you learn?

   _____

   _____

   _____

   _____

Don't Let Fear Limit Your Vision

Roy T. Bennett (2021), in *The Light in the Heart,* said that…

Strong people have a strong sense of self-worth and self-awareness; they don't need the approval of others.

In the spaces that follow, explore the people from whom you seek approval, why the person's approval is so vital to you, and how you can begin to reduce the need for their approval. Some tips for reducing your need for the approval of others are included at the bottom of the page.

People Whose Approval I Seek	Why This Approval Is Vital to Me	How I Can Begin to Reduce My Need for Their Approval
Example: My work supervisor.	*Her evaluation affects my salary. I attach my self-worth to how much money I make.*	*I can work on disconnecting my sense of worth from what I earn.*

Ways to reduce your need for the approval of others:
- Replace the critical voice in your head with a compassionate voice.
- Surround yourself with people who have your best interests at heart.
- Check the accuracy of your beliefs and revise them when necessary.
- Try to understand why you constantly seek the approval of others.
- Write down five accomplishments every evening.
- Keep your goals realistic and attainable.

Solicit Feedback from Others

Many people do not realize how unique and special they are. Chances are that you may not see yourself as others see you. It may be difficult to get a sense of your self-worth without hearing positive feedback from others.

In the boxes below, list what you believe to be five of your most meaningful qualities.

Connect with another person, and ask them to name what they think are your five most meaningful qualities.

Now, compare the two!

Level 1 Journaling

The following journaling prompts encourage personal self-discovery. ***For each prompt, analyze central concepts of what you have learned by completing the therapeutic plan materials in this chapter.***

What is self-worth, and how does it manifest in your daily life? Provide an example.

_____

_____

_____

_____

_____

_____

_____

_____

What is the connection between self-worth and meaning in life?

_____

_____

_____

_____

_____

_____

_____

_____

What are some ways to enhance self-worth?

_____

_____

_____

_____

_____

_____

_____

_____

Level 2 Journaling

The following journaling prompts are reflective to help you develop metacognitive skills, increasing awareness of your learning processes by contemplating what you learned and how you learned it. *For each prompt, analyze central concepts of what you have learned by completing the therapeutic plan materials in this chapter.*

Reflect on a time when you had very positive self-worth. What proceeded this feeling?

_____

_____

_____

_____

_____

_____

_____

_____

How is your self-worth tied to questions like, "Why am I here?" and "Who am I?"

_____

_____

_____

_____

_____

_____

_____

_____

How is your thinking influenced by your sense of self-worth, and vice versa?

_____

_____

_____

_____

_____

_____

_____

Level 3 Journaling

The following journaling prompts promote the development of wisdom by asking you to implement metacognitive skills in your daily life. ***For each prompt, analyze central concepts of what you have learned by completing the therapeutic plan materials in this chapter.***

Describe how you will enhance your sense of self-worth in your work life and family life.

_____

_____

_____

_____

_____

_____

_____

_____

_____

What types of changes will you make so that you experience more meaning in your life?

_____

_____

_____

_____

_____

_____

_____

_____

_____

How does using your strengths and values influence your self-worth? How will you rely more on your strengths and values in choosing which activities to participate in?

_____

_____

_____

_____

_____

_____

_____

_____

_____

CHAPTER 5

Make Meaning by Doing Things for Others

Chapter 5 Therapeutic Plan

Goals
- Participants will learn the importance of doing for others to enhance meaning.
- Participants will be able to identify the connection between serving others and meaning in life.
- Participants will learn how to engage fully in activities that provide meaning through being of service to others.

Actions
- Facilitators will explain and lead discussions about the importance of doing for others to increase meaning in life.
- Facilitators should use each classroom, group situation, or one-on-one client session to structure and administer one or more worksheets to participants.
- Allow participants plenty of time to complete the worksheet.
- Participants can get into smaller groups or pairs to discuss their responses to the activities.
- At this time, participants can move into the larger group to provide opportunities to share their findings. Please remind all participants that they do not have to share anything they do not want to discuss. This space provides room for individuals to reflect; however, there is no obligation to do so.
- Individuals can share their self-discoveries with a trusted professional.

Demonstrations of Learning
- Journaling activities will help determine how much your participants have learned and if they have achieved their goals.
- Journaling activities at the end of each chapter should be given as homework assignments. Facilitators can administer the journaling activities near the beginning (Level 1 Journaling), in the middle (Level 2 Journaling), and near the end (Level 3 Journaling).
- As stated in the Introduction, facilitators can determine if and how to grade the journal entries.

Environment
- Move the seats into a large group, then break into smaller groups or pairs as necessary. When working with an individual client, create a comfortable, neutral environment.
- Download and print exercises from the workbook that are related to your specific topics.

Learn About Social Issues

One of the first things you can do to add meaning to your life is learn about the different social issues in your community or country.

To complete this page, identify and research the social issues you are interested in and want to help with. Place a checkmark in front of the ones of interest. If the issue is not listed, use the "other" line at the end to describe an issue you have researched and found interesting. Then, rank order the ones you checked.

- ☐ _____ Homelessness
- ☐ _____ Climate Change
- ☐ _____ Overpopulation
- ☐ _____ Economic Inequality and Poverty
- ☐ _____ Illiteracy and Lack of Education
- ☐ _____ Gender Inequality
- ☐ _____ Refugees and Immigration
- ☐ _____ Health Care Availability
- ☐ _____ Poverty
- ☐ _____ Racism
- ☐ _____ Reproductive Rights
- ☐ _____ Gun Control
- ☐ _____ Obesity
- ☐ _____ Animal Rights
- ☐ _____ Social Justice
- ☐ _____ Pollution
- ☐ _____ War
- ☐ _____ Unemployment
- ☐ _____ Indigenous Rights
- ☐ _____ Criminal Justice Reform
- ☐ _____ Access to Education
- ☐ _____ Mental Health Issues
- ☐ _____ Other:_____
- ☐ _____ Other:_____

How can you get started to help with the issue you ranked first?

_____

_____

_____

What is one long-term and one short-term goal you have for helping with this social issue?

_____

_____

_____

Let Me Bring... (Page 1)

Read the excerpt from The Prayer of St. Francis (1912) and answer the questions below.

Where there is hatred, let me bring love,

Where there is offense, let me bring pardon,

Where there is discord, let me bring union,

Where there is error, let me bring truth,

Where there is doubt, let me bring hope,

Where there is darkness, let me bring light,

Where there is sadness, let me bring joy,

because it is in giving of oneself that one receives,

it is in forgetting oneself that one is found.

Where is there hatred, and how will you bring love to the people in the situation?

_____

_____

_____

Where is there offense, and how will you bring pardon to the situation?

_____

_____

_____

Where is there discord, and how will you bring union to the people?

_____

_____

_____

Where is there error, and how will you bring truth to right the wrong?

_____

_____

_____

(Continued on the next page)

Let Me Bring... (Page 2)

Read the excerpt from The Prayer of St. Francis (1912) and answer the questions below.

Where there is hatred, let me bring love,

Where there is offense, let me bring pardon,

Where there is discord, let me bring union,

Where there is error, let me bring truth,

Where there is doubt, let me bring hope,

Where there is darkness, let me bring light,

Where there is sadness, let me bring joy,

because it is in giving of oneself that one receives,

it is in forgetting oneself that one is found.

Where is there doubt, and how will you bring hope?

_____

_____

_____

Where is their darkness, and how will you bring light to illuminate the problem?

_____

_____

_____

Where is there sadness, and how will you bring joy to help the people?

_____

_____

_____

What does *"because it is in giving oneself that one receives, it is in forgetting oneself that one is found"* mean to you?

_____

_____

_____

I Can Donate

It's no great secret that giving to others improves our feelings of purpose and meaning. Giving can take many forms: donating your time, material goods, talents, money… ***In each of the four boxes, write, doodle, or draw about what you could do for others who need your help.***

I can donate my time to help others by…	I can donate my material goods to help others by…
I can donate my talents to help others by…	**I can donate my money to help others by…**

Helping the People in My Life

Psychologist Carol Ryff (2014) was among the first to discover the significant link between a meaningful life and helping others. She determined that people create meaning through action rather than stumbling upon it. It starts with looking for ways to help others. A great place to begin is by helping people in your life. For example, you could help your sister move furniture, help your friend fix a broken door, *help your neighbor take groceries into the house, or help a coworker conduct a research study.*

People in My Life	How I Will Be Helpful
Family Members	
Special Friends and Intimate Partners	
Acquaintances	
People You Work With	
Neighbors	
People in the Community	
Other Students	
Others	

Helping People in My Community

Altruism – A principle or practice of selfless concern for other people or animals and working to improve their lives.

Altruistic people search for ways to benefit others. Through benefiting others, they enhance their own well-being. How can you help? Perhaps you can volunteer at your local soup kitchen, help clean a nearby park, or engage with a community sports club that promotes physical activity. ***In the following spaces, list some ways you help in your community and some ways you want to begin helping.***

Ways I Am Helping   **Ways I Want to Begin Helping**

_____

_____

_____

_____

_____

_____

Now pick one of the ways you listed that you want to begin helping: _____

What is one positive action you can take to get started?

_____

_____

_____

Helping the Earth

Some people find meaning in helping with significant issues, such as the harmful effects of climate change. What types of things can you begin doing to slow changes in the climate and help preserve the natural environment? *In the table that follows, list the things you will begin doing to ensure that the natural environment survives to be enjoyed by future generations*.

How I Can Help Climate Change and Preserve Nature	How I Can Help	How This Will Help the World
Example: Recycle.	*I started saving aluminum cans and taking them to the recycling center.*	*It reduces pollution and saves energy.*
Recycle		
Use Clean Green Energy		
Rethink Transportation		
Buy Less		
Use Fewer Plastic Products		
Grow Your Own Food		
Write to Elected Officials		
Other		
Other		
Other		

Contribution Quote

You are developing certain gifts and talents that you can later use to contribute to society.

Help others and give something back. I guarantee you will discover that while public service improves the lives and the world around you, its greatest reward is the enrichment and new meaning it will bring your own life.
~ Arnold Schwarzenegger

Answer the following questions related to this quote:

What are your greatest gifts and talents?

_____

_____

_____

What do you want to contribute?

_____

_____

_____

How can you help others in your community?

_____

_____

_____

How can you improve the lives of others in the world?

_____

_____

_____

How will helping others bring new meaning to your life?

_____

_____

_____

Serving the World (Page 1)

You can use your gifts and talents in many different ways to enhance your sense of meaning in life. A direct correlation exists between serving the world and your sense of meaning. How do you want to use your gifts and talents to serve the world? *In the spaces that follow, identify how you might use your gifts and talents.*

My Gifts/Talents: _____

_____

How I Will Serve the World

Place a checkmark in front of the ways you might serve the world. On the lines, journal about how you might leverage your gifts and talents to serve people.

☐ **Create Things**
Many people are very creative and innovative and can take materials available and work with them to create a new product to sell to their customers. They are good at producing products that people need and are willing to pay for. How could you do this?

_____

_____

☐ **Sell Things**
Many business owners are good at selling products they make or get from others. They tend to be self-directed, people-oriented, assertive in selling their products, and persevering in the face of rejection. How could you do this?

_____

_____

☐ **Repair or Build Things**
Many people enjoy working with their hands doing manual hands-on work. They are driven to build something tangible where nothing exists or repair things to make them run more efficiently or smoothly. How could you do this?

_____

_____

☐ **Communicate About Things**
There are many options for people who communicate clearly. They can communicate one-on-one, in small groups, through public speaking, or via media such as television, films, radio, audio, blogs, and websites. How could you do this?

_____

_____

(Continued on the next page)

Serving the World (Page 2)

You can use your gifts and talents in many different ways to enhance your sense of meaning in life. A direct correlation exists between serving the world and your sense of meaning. How do you want to use your gifts and talents to serve the world? ***In the spaces that follow, identify how you might use your gifts and talents***.

My Gifts/Talents: _____

_____

☐ **Understand Things**
Many people are happiest when they are trying to understand things. They are curious and want to figure things out and learn how they work. They enjoy tinkering with new technology and playing with new equipment. How could you do this?

_____

_____

☐ **Organize Things**
Many people are proficient at organizing systems or people. They tend to work with numbers and manage human and physical resources well. They are attentive to details and good at meeting deadlines. How could you do this?

_____

_____

☐ **Care for Things**
Many people know there is a huge need to care for other people, animals, things, plants, and the earth. They are nurturing, supportive, caring, helpful, and interested in finding ways to help others who need care. How could you do this?

_____

_____

☐ **Entertain**
Many people prefer to work with others and enjoy making them feel welcome and happy. They want to ensure that people are having a good time and being entertained. How could you do this?

_____

_____

☐ **Teach**
Many people want to work where they can use their training and teaching skills to help others learn new skills or improve existing ones. How could you do this?

_____

_____

Random Acts of Kindness

Facts about random acts of kindness:
- They are acts performed by a person wishing to help or positively affect another person.
- They are kind acts you do for someone you may not know.
- They are doing something nice for someone else "just because you want to."
- They are not undertaken to repay others or because you have to. They are done because you want to help others.
- They do not need to be for the same person; the person doesn't even have to know that you are doing them.

People who do random acts of kindness for others often feel happier and report that their life is more meaningful. Over this week, perform five random acts of kindness. It doesn't matter if the acts are big or small. It is more powerful if you perform a variety of acts. *Examples include feeding a stranger's parking meter, picking up litter, helping a friend with a chore, giving someone a ride, baking someone a cake, or providing a meal to someone in need.* **Write your random acts of kindness below. After each act, write down what you did in at least one or two sentences, and then write how it made you feel.**

Random Acts of Kindness	What I did	How It Made Me Feel

How do these types of acts provide your life with meaning?

_____

_____

From Pain Comes Compassion

All people search for meaning in their lives. For most people, meaning comes from:
- Experiencing relationships with significant others.
- Helping others live better lives.
- Making significant contributions to society.

For many people, the ability to turn a negative experience of pain into a benefit to others provides a tremendous sense of meaning.

Think about how you have experienced pain and yet were able to grow. Then describe how you used this pain to be compassionate toward others (or would like to use it to be compassionate toward others).

My Pain	How I Learned and Grew	How I Used This Knowledge or How I Could Use It
Example: My son committed suicide when I was younger.	I have dedicated my life to learning about the causes of suicide.	I am now volunteering as a mental health advocate at the Department of Social Services.

How has helping others provided your life with more meaning?

_____

_____

_____

The purpose of human life is to serve, and to show compassion and the will to help others.
~ Albert Schweitzer

Connecting With Others

Helping others can help you connect to people. Because humans are social beings, connections can bring meaning to your life. Helping others can help you form relationships, strengthen social connections, and add meaning. The more people you help, the bigger your support network becomes – your network grows as you build new relationships. ***In the spaces below, please describe how you have helped others, how it has grown your social network, and added meaning to your life.***

How I Have Helped Others	How It Added to My Social Network	How It Helped Bring More Meaning to My Life
Example: I volunteered at the local animal shelter.	*I met some amazing people who were also volunteering their time.*	*I love helping others, and many volunteers have formed a social group to help animals on a larger scale.*

Things to Remember:
- Helping others is something you can do daily.
- As you pay attention to your neighborhood, you will realize that many people suffer from emotional pain, mental illness, loss, or other life challenges. They might benefit from your help.
- Many people don't know how to ask for help, so be alert for opportunities to help others.
- Try to do a good deed or practice acts of kindness daily.

Show Appreciation for Others

Doing for others by showing appreciation is an often overlooked way to find meaning in life. Everyone wants to be appreciated. Many people feel unappreciated by those around them. It is important to take time to tell people what you appreciate about them.

Example: "You know, I've always appreciated your generosity and the way you show it by bringing me baked goods when I'm feeling down."

Now write about who you appreciate and why. When you give people positive, appreciative feedback regularly, you help them see the best in themselves.

I appreciate _____ for: _____

_____

I appreciate _____ for: _____

_____

I appreciate _____ for: _____

_____

I appreciate _____ for: _____

_____

I appreciate _____ for: _____

_____

I appreciate _____ for: _____

_____

I appreciate _____ for: _____

_____

Now decide how you will tell each person how much you appreciate them.

Level 1 Journaling

The following journaling prompts encourage personal self-discovery. *For each prompt, analyze central concepts of what you have learned by completing the therapeutic plan materials in this chapter.*

What does "doing for others" mean to you?

_____

_____

_____

_____

_____

_____

_____

_____

What do you think the connection is between meaning and doing for others?

_____

_____

_____

_____

_____

_____

_____

_____

What have you learned about yourself and your interest in doing for others?

_____

_____

_____

_____

_____

_____

_____

_____

Level 2 Journaling

The following journaling prompts are reflective to help you develop metacognitive skills, increasing awareness of your learning processes by contemplating what you learned and how you learned it. *For each prompt, analyze central concepts of what you have learned by completing the therapeutic plan materials in this chapter.*

Reflect on how you feel when you help others. How does this help you better understand your purpose in life?

_____

_____

_____

_____

_____

_____

_____

Who are some of the people you want to help more? Why do you want to help them?

_____

_____

_____

_____

_____

_____

_____

Are you more interested in helping people in your community, state, country, or the world? Why?

_____

_____

_____

_____

_____

_____

_____

Level 3 Journaling

The following journaling prompts promote the development of wisdom by asking you to implement metacognitive skills in your daily life. ***For each prompt, analyze central concepts of what you have learned by completing the therapeutic plan materials in this chapter.***

What steps will you take to begin doing more for others? Describe them.

_____

_____

_____

_____

_____

_____

_____

Describe one long-term (for the next five years) and one short-term (for the next month) goal you have to begin doing for others.

_____

_____

_____

_____

_____

_____

_____

How will you integrate your desire to serve into your daily schedule and routine?

_____

_____

_____

_____

_____

_____

_____

References

Ackerman, C. E. (2018). *What is the meaning of life according to positive psychology?* Positive Psychology. positivepsychology.com/meaning-of-life-positive-psychology/

Beck, A. T. (1967). *Depression: Clinical, experimental, and theoretical aspects.* Hoeber Medical Division.

Bennett, R. T. (2021). *The light in the heart: Inspirational thoughts for living your best life.* Self-Published.

De Shazer, S., Berg, I. K., Lipchik, E., Nunnally, E., Molnar, A., Gingerich, W., & Weiner-Davis, M. (1986). Brief therapy: Focused solution development. *Family Process,* 25(2): 207–221.

Edey, W., Jevne, R. F., & Westra, K. (1998). Key elements of hope-focused counselling: The art of making hope visible. *Hope Foundation of Alberta.*

Frankl, V. E. (2006). *Man's search for meaning.* Beacon Press.

Hayes, S. C., & Lillis, J. (2012). Acceptance and commitment therapy. *American Psychological Association.*

Klerman G. L., DiMascio A., Weissman M., Prusoff B., & Paykel E. S. (1974). Treatment of depression by drugs and psychotherapy. *The American Journal of Psychiatry,* 131(186–191).

Linehan, M. M. (1993). *Doing dialectical behavior therapy.* Guilford Press.

Lewinsohn, P. M. & Shaffer M. (1971). Use of home observations as an integral part of the treatment of depression: Preliminary report and case studies. *Journal of Consulting and Clinical Psychology,* 37 (87–94).

Leutenberg, E. R. A., & Liptak, J. J. (2016). *The journey to transcendence teen workbook.* Bureau for At-Risk Youth.

Madeson, M. (2017). *Seligman's PERMA+ model explained: A theory of wellbeing.* Positive Psychology. positivepsychology.com/perma-model/

Prayer of St. Francis (1912) La Clochette. The holy mass league, Father Esther Bouquerel. loyolapress.com/catholic-resources/prayer/traditional-catholic-prayers/saints-prayers/peace-prayer-of-saint-francis/

Reker, G. T., & Wong, P. T. P. (1988). Personal meaning in life and psychosocial adaptation in the later years. In P. T. P. Wong (Ed.), *The human quest for meaning: Theories, research, and applications* (2nd ed., pp. 433-456). Routledge.

Rusk, R. & Waters, D. (2015). A psycho-social system approach to well-being: Empirically deriving the five domains of positive functioning. *The Journal of Positive Psychology,* 10(2), 141-152.

Scallon, M., & Liptak, J. (2021). *Cognitive flexibility.* E-Book PDF. bookboon.com/en/cognitive-flexibility-ebook

Seligman, M. (2018). PERMA and the building blocks of well-being. *The Journal of Positive Psychology,* 13(4), 333-335.

Seligman, M. E. (2012). *Flourish: A visionary new understanding of happiness and well-being.* Atria Paperback.

Seligman, M. (2008, July). The new era of positive psychology [Video]. TED Conferences.

Snyder, C. R., Irving, L. M., & Anderson, J. R. (1991). Hope and health. In C. R. Snyder & D. R. Forsyth (Eds.), *Handbook of social and clinical psychology: The health perspective* (pp. 285–305). Pergamon Press.

About the Authors

Dr. Michelle J. Scallon earned her doctoral degree in Clinical Psychology from Seattle Pacific University (SPU) in 2007. She earned her BA in Psychology with a minor in Business from Central Washington University and her Master's Degree in Psychology from SPU. Dr. Scallon conducted a research study while completing her dissertation titled *The Impact of Social Support and Humor on Levels of Hope in Individuals Who Are Coping With HIV/AIDS*. In addition to this research, she made peer-reviewed presentations at the Western Psychological Association conference in Palm Springs, CA. She has presented research on cognitive flexibility, coping, and hope in the HIV/AIDS population.

Dr. Scallon has over 15 years of experience providing counseling and psychotherapy to a wide variety of populations. For over ten years, she worked as a mental health clinician and supervisor in a correctional institution, treating incarcerated individuals and conducting therapeutic groups. Dr. Scallon conducted crisis work and psychotherapy and was integral to running a mental health program called Modified Therapeutic Community. This program was aimed at helping incarcerated individuals increase prosocial skills to reduce their chances of recidivism.

Dr. Scallon draws on a wide variety of evidence-based techniques, including those from Positive Psychology. Since the beginning of the COVID-19 pandemic, she has become an internationally known self-help author. She has written sixteen books, many with Dr. John Liptak. She is passionate about helping people capitalize on their strengths to maintain hope. Her current interest is finding ways to help people remain positive and cope amidst the challenges of personal and global change. In her spare time, she is an avid volunteer for a local children's non-profit organization.

◆ ❖ ◆

Dr. John J. Liptak is an internationally recognized author with over thirty years of work experience providing counseling services for mental health clients, college students, offenders, and ex-offenders. He has spent a lifetime developing hope-generating materials for others to use. He authored over 100 workbooks with Ester Leutenberg on topics such as stress management, substance abuse, domestic violence, and developing and maintaining effective personal and intimate relationships. In addition, John has written 31 career assessment instruments for JIST Publishing, ten books for various publishers, and13 e-books for Bookboon.

Dr. Liptak is the President of the Center for Career Assessment, Inc., a research and development firm specializing in creating hope-related psychoeducational materials. He works with multiple publishing firms. The materials he developed are used internationally in a wide variety of settings, including schools, job training centers, mental health facilities, and prisons.

John's work has been featured in the Associated Press and in numerous newspapers, including *The Washington Post, Tampa Bay Times,* and *The Pittsburgh Post-Gazette,* on MSNBC television and CNN radio. He appeared in the PAX/ION television series *Success Without a College Degree.* John earned a Doctor of Education in Counselor Education/School Counseling and Guidance from Virginia Tech. He lives in Radford, Virginia, with his wife Kathy and their Shih Tzu named MacKenzie.

WholePerson

Whole Person Associates is a leading publisher of training resources for professionals who empower people to create and maintain healthy lifestyles. Our creative resources will help you work effectively with your clients in the areas of stress management, wellness promotion, mental health, and life skills.

Please visit us at our website: **WholePerson.com**. You can check out our entire line of products, place an order, request our print catalog, and sign up for our monthly special notifications.

Whole Person Associates
800-247-6789
Books@WholePerson.com

Positive Psychology – The Hope Series

Discover and Create Meaning in Your Life
Generate a Sense of Accomplishment in Your Life
Maintain Positive, Healthy Relationships in Your Life
Regain Control in Your Life
Cultivate Hope and Engagement in your Life

Free PDF Download Available

To access your free PDF download of the exercises in this workbook, go to:

https://WholePerson.com/store/DiscoverandCreateMeaning2001.html

Printed in the USA
CPSIA information can be obtained
at www.ICGtesting.com
CBHW080854190324
5543CB00003B/9